PRIMARY ACTIVITY BOX

Games and activities for younger learners

Caroline Nixon
and Michael Tomlinson

CAMBRIDGE
UNIVERSITY PRESS

PUBLISHED BY THE PRESS SYNDICATE OF THE UNIVERSITY OF CAMBRIDGE
The Pitt Building, Trumpington Street, Cambridge, United Kingdom

CAMBRIDGE UNIVERSITY PRESS
The Edinburgh Building, Cambridge CB2 2RU, UK
40 West 20th Street, New York, NY 10011–4211, USA
477 Williamstown Road, Port Melbourne, VIC 3207, Australia
Ruiz de Alarcón 13, 28014 Madrid, Spain
Dock House, The Waterfront, Cape Town 8001, South Africa

http://www.cambridge.org

First published 2001
Third printing 2002

Printed in the United Kingdom at the University Press, Cambridge

Typeface Futura 9.5/13pt.   *System* QuarkXPress®   [GECKO]

A catalogue for this book is available from the British Library

ISBN 0 521 77941 3 Resource Book
ISBN 0 521 77966 9 Cassette

PRIMARY ACTIVITY BOX

Contents

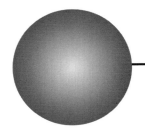

Thanks and acknowledgements

We would like to give special thanks to the following people:
To Alison Sharpe and Bella Wigan for their vision and faith.
To Nóirín Burke and Alyson Maskell for their sound judgement and excellent guidance.
To Ricardo and Paloma for all their practical help and encouragement.
To James Kelly and Siobhan McNiece and our pupils at Star English, Murcia, Spain for thoroughly trialling the material at all stages, and for offering invaluable advice and suggestions.

We would like to thank the following teachers for their helpful suggestions as a result of trialling or commenting on the manuscript in its draft form:

Aileen Anderson, Madrid, Spain; Karen A Anythana, Bangkok, Thailand; Jaime Carrera, Santiago, Chile; Celia Gasgil, Izmir, Turkey; Yoshie Kobayashi, Yokohama, Kanagawa-ken, Japan; Maria Edvirgem Zeny, Parana, Brazil; Despina Konstantinopoulou, Athens, Greece; Ana María Espina Madariaga, Santiago, Chile; Pamela O'Brien, Madrid, Spain; Ian Reid, Parede, Portugal; Andrea Paul, Melbourne, Australia; Barbara Sciborowska, Warszawa, Poland; Liz Soydas, Izmir, Turkey; Roma Starczewska, Taipei, Taiwan; Magdalena Szpotwicz, Komorow, Poland; Mark Thompson, Bangkok, Thailand; Su-Wei Wang, Taiwan; Belinda Wicks, Bradford on Avon, UK.

Illustrations: Kathy Baxendale (pp. 107, 115, 127); Carey Bennett (pp. 15, 17, 37, 47, 65); Becky Blake (pp. 102, 117); Lizzy Finlay (pp. 90, 91); Gecko DTP (pp. 13, 21, 79, 122); Sue Hendra (pp. 25, 35, 81, 123); Lorna Kent (pp. 33, 40, 41, 61, 103, 105); Melanie Mansfield (pp. 31, 57, 93, 94, 127); Nick Schon (pp. 59, 69); Martin Shovel (pp. 29, 113); Lisa Smith (pp. 9, 20, 23, 73, 75, 85, 86, 89, 92, 96, 97, 106, 111); Kay Widdowson (pp. 63, 67, 77, 99, 100); Lisa Williams (pp. 71, 87, 88); Celia Witchard (p. 43)

Photographs: Jeremy Pembrey (p. 128)
Text design: Dave Seabourne
Page make up: Gecko Ltd.
Cover illustration: Barbara Vagnozzi
Cassette
The cassette was produced by Tim Douglass (music) and Tony Garside (speech) of Forum Productions.

Our thanks also go to the following children who sing on the cassette and the teachers who rehearsed them:

Helen Teanby and children from Albourne C.E. School, Brighton:
Toby Mew; Rosie-Jo MacRae; Leanne Capel; Kara Wheeler; Joseph Hoare; Hayley Walker; Aramis Gorriette; Hector Gwynne; Thomas Hinton; Sam Murray; Martin Hays-Nowak; Hannah Cutress; Priscilla Barker; Luke Norris; Daniel Levene; Charlotte West; Elliot Wise; Louis Brooks; Charlie Lennon; Lottie Hazel; Bethan Zeidler

Robbie Mitchell and children from Varndean School, Brighton:
Kellie Tamkin; Natalie Godfrey; Polly Rae Smith; Danielle Blance; Mila Stojanovic; Lizzie Hunt; Rachel Francis; Charlotte Hailey-Watts; Lindsey Walford; Hannah Osmond-Smith; Emma Simmonds; Rebecca Swannack; Emily Blair; Laura Hughes; Amy Beton; Suzy Grace; Jess Hovell; Gabriella Benton-Stace; Eleanor Rosenbach; Katie Spedding; Ella Scott; Rebecca Tamkin; Anna Brooks; Flora Scott; Amy Hicks

Dedication
I would like to dedicate this book to Doctor Escribano and Doctor Villaverde of the Hospital Vírgen de la Arrixaca for their excellent medical care and humanity, and to Pedro Martínez for his hard work and infinite patience.
Caroline Nixon

Part of the proceeds from this book are being given to *Médecins Sans Frontières*.

Map of the Book

Activity title	Activity type	Language focus	Level	Age	Skills focus	Time
4 Pronunciation						
4.1 Legs! Legs! Legs!	Individual reading and pronunciation puzzle	Sound recognition /e/ and /iː/	3	9–11	Reading, listening	20–40
4.2 Rhyming words	Individual pronunciation activity	Pronunciation: rhyming words	2	7–10	Pronunciation	40–50
4.3 Fabulous phonicolours	Individual pronunciation activity	Pronunciation of simple vocabulary	2	9–11	Reading	20–40
4.4 Space race	Pairwork pronunciation activity	Recognition of /eɪ/ sound	3	10–11	Reading, speaking	20–30
5 Communication practice						
5.1 In your classroom who ...?	Class survey: information gap activity	Are you ...? Can you ...? Have you got ...?	2	8–11	Speaking, listening, reading, writing	30
5.2 Identikit	Pairwork information gap activity	Have/Has got, parts of the body, adjectives	2	8–11	Speaking, listening, reading, writing (optional)	20–30
5.3 They can do it	Pairwork information gap activity	Can/can't: questions and short answers	2	8–11	Speaking, listening, reading, writing (optional)	20–30
5.4 Room for improvement	Pairwork 'spot the difference' activity	There is/are, prepositions of place, bedroom objects	3	9–11	Speaking, listening, writing (optional)	50
5.5 You read, I write	Pairwork dictation	To be, have got, physical description	2	8–10	Reading, listening, speaking	20–30
5.6 Colour co-ordinates	Pairwork information gap activity	Have got: questions and short answers, clothes and colours	2	7–11	Speaking, listening, reading, writing (optional)	30
6 Playtime						
6.1 Whose is it?	Individual matching exercise	Possessive 's, Whose?, classroom objects	1	5–8	Speaking, writing (optional)	20–30
6.2 Gramminoes	Pairwork or small group dominoes game	Personal pronouns, to be, simple adjectives	2	8–11	Reading, speaking, writing (optional)	20
6.3 Which sweet?	Individual question and answer matching	Question words with verb to be	3	7–10	Reading	20
6.4 Sentence Bingo	Whole class Bingo game	To be, have, can, toys, age, appearance	2	7–9	Listening, reading	30–40
6.5 Cowboy dot-to-dot	Individual 'join the dots' dictation	Present continuous	2	8–10	Reading, listening, writing, speaking	30–45

Activity title	Activity type	Language focus	Level	Age	Skills focus	Time
7 Rhyme time						
7.1 Jack and Jill	Song, individual 'listen and colour'	Clothes, colours, possessive 's	1	5–8	Listening, speaking	50–60
7.2 Incy Wincy Spider	Action song, individual sequencing activity, 'read and colour'	Weather vocabulary	2	7–9	Listening, speaking, reading	50–60
7.3 Lucy Locket	Action rhyme, individual sound differentiation activity	Basic vocabulary and pronunciation of /ɒ/, /ɔː/, /ɜː/, /iː/	2	7–10	Listening, speaking, reading, writing	50–60
7.4 My fish tank	Song, individual 'make and do' activity	Numbers 1–10, colours, *left, right*	1	5–8	Listening, speaking, reading	45
7.5 Diddle diddle dumpling	Rhyme, individual sound differentiation activity	Sound recognition: /ɒ/, /aʊ/, /uː/	3	8–11	Speaking, listening, reading, writing	20–30
8 Make and do						
8.1 Farmyard fun	Song, whole class dictation, pairwork activity	Animals, *there is/are* or *has got*	1	5–8	Listening, speaking, writing (optional)	60
8.2 Two little dicky birds	Rhyme with puppets: whole class and pairwork	Classroom instructions	1	6–9	Listening, speaking	50
8.3 Chatterboxes	Individual 'make and do' activity, pairwork practice	Numbers 1–10, colours, adjectives, *as* for comparison	3	8–11	Writing, listening, speaking	45
8.4 Days and dates	Rhyme, individual activity – making a calendar	Days, months	2	8–11	Listening, writing	50
8.5 Dress me up	Whole class dictation, pairwork information gap	Clothes	1	5–9	Listening, speaking, writing (optional)	60
9 Problem solving						
9.1 DIY wordsearch	Individual or small group wordsearch	Any lexical groups	1–3	8–11	Reading, writing	30–40
9.2 Where are they sitting?	Individual cognitive puzzle, information transfer	*Can, next to, between, on the left/right*	2	9–11	Reading, writing (optional), listening (optional)	30
9.3 Dotty's puppies	Individual cognitive puzzle, information transfer	*have got, long, short, fat, thin, big, small*	3	9–11	Reading, writing, listening, speaking (optional)	45
9.4 Broken words	Individual vocabulary matching	Months, days, seasons	2	8–11	Reading, writing	40
9.5 Shaping up	Individual 'read and colour' or 'listen and colour' activity	Comparatives, superlatives, shapes, colours, *in, inside*	3	9–11	Reading or listening, writing (optional)	30

Answer key to activities 2.5, 4.3, 7.3, 9.2

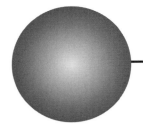

Introduction

What is *Primary Activity Box*?

Primary Activity Box is a resource book of supplementary activities for young learners (5–11 years approximately), containing photocopiable worksheets. The intention is to provide both teacher and pupil with enjoyable activities which will make teaching and learning fun. The activities include songs, rhymes, puzzles and games for listening, speaking, reading and writing. They are designed to suit a variety of learning and teaching styles, with elements of language acquisition through body movement, visual and audio approaches. The lexical and grammatical content reflect the syllabus of most Primary EFL coursebooks and there are also traditional English rhymes, songs and games.

The activities are of different lengths, ranging from ten-minute gap-fillers through to 'make and do' activities that may occupy the greater part of the lesson. There are task-based activities, where pupils use English as the vehicle to find the answer to a task or problem without necessarily thinking consciously about the language they are using. This challenge can be highly stimulating for the younger learner. Emphasis has been placed upon the use of puzzles and games, quite simply because they are fun to do. Some of the activities incorporate an element of competition which can be highly motivating for younger learners as it leads them to use grammatical structures more enthusiastically, and increases their desire to do so correctly.

Who is *Primary Activity Box* for?

Age range

At all times we have tried to bear in mind the specific needs of the different age groups within the five to eleven-year-old range. The needs of those five to seven-year-olds who cannot yet read or write confidently contrast sharply with those of eight to eleven-year-olds who need a more challenging type of activity. For each activity, we suggest the age range for which it is suitable; we give quite a wide age range because children's capacity to do any particular activity will depend largely on their first language, cultural background and the length of time they have been learning English. Whereas some of the activities are aimed at one or the other end of the age range, we have also tried to offer flexibility within these parameters. For example, younger learners might do only the oral part of an activity, while older or more competent learners could do the whole activity. In all cases teachers themselves are the best judges of their pupils' ability to carry out an activity successfully, irrespective of their age.

The time it takes to do an activity will also vary with the age and ability of the pupils. The amount of time we recommend for each activity should be taken to be the most that a class at the younger end of the age range would need.

Level

We have organised the activities in *Primary Activity Box* into three levels. This is intended as a guide to the language abilities pupils will need in order to do the activities. These levels do not refer to any wider EFL standards.

Level 1 is intended for learners with a knowledge of basic vocabulary (numbers, colours, adjectives, nouns, simple prepositions) without much grammatical structure. Here the main emphasis is on an oral presentation for pupils with few or no reading and writing skills.

Level 2 is intended for learners with a knowledge of wider lexical groups with the verbs *to be, to have, can* and some basic verbs in the simple present and present continuous tenses. There is an integration of all four skills with slightly more emphasis on the oral aspect for pupils with limited reading and writing skills.

Level 3 is intended for learners with a firmer grasp of the knowledge included above and the ability to use grammatical structures more competently as tools for reading, writing and speaking.

We have tried to offer suggestions where possible for weaker readers, non-Roman alphabet learners or non-readers and we also suggest extension activities for more advanced learners or fast finishers.

The templates at the back of the book enable teachers to devise their own version of some activities or to allow learners to create their own. In this way teachers can adapt an activity to the specific needs of their class and coursebook.

When to use *Primary Activity Box*

The activities can be used as extra material to back up a coursebook. Likewise they can be used for revision and reinforcement. They are ideal for teachers who work without a coursebook. They can be used on those days when it is not a good idea to start a new topic: the day before a bank holiday, Christmas or Easter, days of high absenteeism due to bouts of illness or extra-curricular activities, etc. They are useful for teachers who have to stand in when the class teacher is absent.

Using *Primary Activity Box* – tips for teachers

The following suggestions are based on our own experience in the classroom. They are by no means definitive and aim simply to give a few teaching ideas to less experienced teachers.

Noise

• Some activities, especially those that involve pupils speaking and moving around in the classroom, will generate a lot of excitement. In the book we use the symbol below to indicate this type of activity. When children are excited they tend to be very noisy and may even lapse into their first language to talk about or discuss some aspect of the activity. Although it can be difficult to get used to at first, noise in the classroom is tolerable if it is related directly to the activity and is an expression of interest or enthusiasm for the task in hand. Regardless of which language they use, if children are sufficiently stimulated by an activity to want to talk about it, then this can only be interpreted as a positive response. You must ensure, however, that only English is used for the completion of specific communication tasks.

Preparation

• The most important thing with any kind of task is to make sure that the pupils have been well prepared beforehand, that they know all the words they will need and that they understand the object of the exercise. Equipping your pupils properly with the necessary linguistic tools to enable them to carry out a task successfully will ensure that it is a challenging and enjoyable one for all. Without the necessary preparation, learners may have a negative learning experience, which will cause them to lose confidence and become frustrated with an activity that, quite simply, they have not got the capacity to do.

• Before starting any activity, demonstrate it first. For pairwork activities choose an individual pupil to help you. Do the first question of the pairwork task with the pupil for the class to get the idea.

When you divide the class into pairs or groups, point to each pupil and say, for example, A – B, A – B, A – B, etc. so they are in no doubt as to what their role is. Try to give simple clear instructions in English. Say, for example, *As ask the question and Bs answer the question: A – B, A – B, A – B. Then Bs ask the question and As answer the question: B – A, B – A, B – A.*

• Always bring a few extra photocopies of the worksheet to avoid tears if any children do it wrong and want to start again.

Classroom dynamics

• Try to move around the classroom while explaining or doing the activities, circulating among your pupils. In this way you project an air of confidence, of being in command and of being more accessible to pupils. Moving around the classroom also enables you more effectively to supervise and monitor pupils who may need more attention at times. Movement in the classroom tends to hold pupils' attention better and makes the class more lively and dynamic.

• In the same way that it is a good idea for teachers to move around, it is also advisable to move the pupils around occasionally. By periodically changing seating arrangements you can help group dynamics and break up potentially disruptive groups. For example, weaker pupils could be put next to stronger ones, and more hard-working pupils next to disruptive ones. Pupils might benefit from working with children they may not usually associate with.

• When forming pairs or groups we suggest that, whenever possible, pupils just move their chairs. For groupwork they can bring their chairs around one or two tables allowing them an easy environment for discussion and written production. For pairwork they can position their two chairs to face each other. This allows a more realistic eye-to-eye communication situation. This change of seating prepares them for the oral work they are about to begin.

• Certain activities in this book can be used to divide the class into random pairs in a more dynamic way. Give pupils a card and ask them to move around the classroom to find their partner. The activities that lend themselves to this are: 3.1 Card games, 3.3 Mix 'n' match, 3.6 Timescales and 6.3 Which sweet?.

Teaching and learning

• Encourage pupils to use their own resources to try to solve a task. Try to guide pupils towards finding the right answers rather than supplying them yourself, even if this means allowing them to make mistakes.

• Making mistakes is a vital part of the learning process, so when pupils are asked to invent their own sentences, stories, etc. we should not expect these to be perfect. Sometimes accuracy must be forfeited for the sake of creativity and enthusiastic participation.

- The Extension activities can be given to those pupils who need an extra task to keep them occupied while the rest of the class finish the main activity. In activities where it is necessary to prepare material, these pupils can be kept busy helping the teacher with cutting out, collecting in and cleaning up.

- Try to avoid the immediate repetition of an activity simply because it has worked well in class and your pupils have enjoyed it. If you do this, the novelty will quickly wear off and children will become bored. Save it for a later occasion and they will come back to it with fresh enthusiasm.

Songs, rhymes and chants

- For the activities based on traditional songs or rhymes it is not important for the learner to understand every word outside the key words to be practised. In these exercises we are more interested in pupils understanding the gist, and we are using the rhyme as a means with which to practise language. The visual aids that accompany each rhyme or song and the actions included in some should provide the learner with sufficient information to be able to understand the overall concept. It is important then, at this stage, not to spend precious class time on lengthy and complicated explanations of specific words.

- Get children to stand up when singing the songs and rhymes. It can make a tremendous difference to their performance and enjoyment.

- The songs, rhymes and chants on the cassette are recorded in several versions: first the complete version; then there is a version with pauses after each line for pupils to repeat in chorus; then there is a version for children to sing, say or chant along with. (The shorter songs and rhymes are sung or said twice at this point.) Finally, for the songs only, there is a 'karaoke' version (music only, no voices) so that pupils can sing the song by themselves. We suggest that you don't try to do the karaoke version in the same lesson as the children learn the song. Wait until a later occasion when the children are really familiar with the song and can sing it confidently.

- All of the songs, rhymes and chants included here can be presented and practised in a variety of different ways to make them more interesting and challenging. These techniques are especially useful if you want to go back to previously practised material for revision or further exploitation and you want to avoid your pupils' reaction of 'We've already done this!'

  - Whisper the rhyme or phrase while clicking your fingers. Repeat the rhyme, getting gradually louder each time, and then reverse the process.
  - Say the rhyme whilst clapping your hands and tapping your foot in time to the rhythm.
  - Divide the class into groups and ask them to repeat the rhyme in rounds. To do this, the first group starts to say the rhyme and then at a suitable point, usually one or two lines into it, the second group starts to say the rhyme from the beginning.
  - Ask your class if anybody wants to do a solo or a duet. The very fact that they are giving a public performance induces most pupils to surpass themselves. It also adds a bit of spice to the proceedings as it gets their adrenaline flowing. If children are reluctant to participate in this however, they should not be forced to do so.
  - With your class tape recorder, record the class saying the rhyme collectively and/or individually. Let your pupils listen to themselves. If they feel that they could improve on the second attempt, record them again. When pupils have sung or said their rhymes into the tape recorder be sure to give them a round of applause and encourage the rest of the class to do the same.
  - If you have access to a video camera and the rhyme you are doing has actions, record your pupils carrying out the activity. As a reward or a treat for their hard work they can then watch themselves.

Display

- Pupils find it extremely motivating to have their work displayed and will generally strive to produce work to the best of their ability if they know it is going to be seen by others. So try to arrange to display pupils' work around the classroom or school whenever possible.

Competition

- An element of competition can make many children try harder. However, while a competition can be a good incentive for an otherwise lazy pupil it can sometimes be demotivating for a less able but ordinarily hardworking one. It is a good idea to balance competitions with other activities to be able to reward or praise individuals according to their different needs and performances.

- Competitions can also lead to a lot of noise and over-enthusiasm in the classroom. Any discipline problems can, however, be curbed by keeping a running total of points on the board and deducting points for shouting out the answer or rowdiness.

Storage of material

- To make the flashcards more attractive and appealing to younger learners it is a good idea to enlarge them, colour them in and laminate them with protective adhesive plastic. In this way you will always have them ready for future use.

- In the same way, it is a good idea to photocopy different sets of the same game onto different coloured card and laminate them with adhesive plastic. These can then be stored for easy retrieval at short notice at a later date.

The last word

We have intended to write a book with which to teach children English in a dynamic, fun, and effective way. We sincerely hope we have achieved this aim and, above all, that you, the teacher, feel that our efforts have been worthwhile.

Caroline Nixon and Michael Tomlinson, Murcia 2001

1.1 PRIMARY ACTIVITY BOX

Happy badges

ACTIVITY TYPE
individual 'make and do'
activity
whole class introductions,
song

LANGUAGE FOCUS
I'm …
I'm a boy/girl.
basic classroom instructions:
cut, stick
question forms:
Are you a boy/girl?
Who are you?
What's your name?

LEVEL
1

AGE RANGE
5–10

SKILLS
speaking, writing

TIME
30–45 minutes

MATERIALS
coloured card (optional), one
safety pin or piece of string
per pupil, sticky tape,
scissors, glue, crayons, one
copy of the *Happy badges*
worksheet per six pupils

Before class
Photocopy the *Happy badges* page onto coloured card, one sheet for every six pupils. Or photocopy it on paper and stick it onto card. Either you or pupils can then colour the badges later. Cut along the dotted lines. Do not cut round the star – pupils will cut them out in the lesson.

In class
1 Introduce yourself, saying *Hi, I'm … .* Ask *Who are you?* Insist on the use of *I'm … .*

2 Write pupils' names on the board as they say them. Make a list of girls' names in one colour and boys' names in another colour. Then ask individual pupils: *Are you a boy? Are you a girl? Are you a boy or a girl?* to elicit the response *I'm a … .* While recognising that these questions are somewhat artificial, they give younger learners more opportunity to talk about themselves, and the teacher has a tool to introduce *he* and *she*.

3 Give each pupil a piece of card with the star on it. Ask them to cut the star out neatly. At this stage be tolerant of different pupils' speeds, offering help where needed.

4 Ask pupils to write their names on their badges. You may wish to give them English versions of their own names.

5 Show pupils how to stick the safety pin onto the badge, then give each pupil their safety pin and sticky tape. Again, help where necessary. With younger learners you may prefer to thread a piece of string through the star, making a medal.

6 Once pupils have made and put on their badges, practise asking their names around the class. You can use either of these Question–Answer formulas:
Who are you? I'm …
What's your name? My name's …
Drill the structures as a class, then individually, and when you think pupils are confident with the structure they can practise it freely. Encourage them to walk around asking other pupils.

7 To end the lesson, teach the class the song *I'm H-A-P-P-Y*. First, pre-teach *happy*. Write it on the board and spell out the letters.

8 Play the song on cassette or sing it. Then pupils repeat it line by line. Finally, they stand up and sing the whole song.

Tapescript
I'm H-A-P-P-Y
I'm H-A-P-P-Y
I know I am
I'm sure I am
I'm H-A-P-P-Y.

Options
1 Pupils can add ages to their badges to produce, for example, *I'm Jim. I'm seven.* and to practise the question *How old are you?*

2 For more advanced pupils, you could enlarge the photocopies so there is room for pupils to write more information about themselves, e.g. *I'm happy, I've got brown hair, I can dance.*

3 For younger learners, you may prefer to write your pupils' names on the stars. Put them on the table and invite them to find their own badges.

12

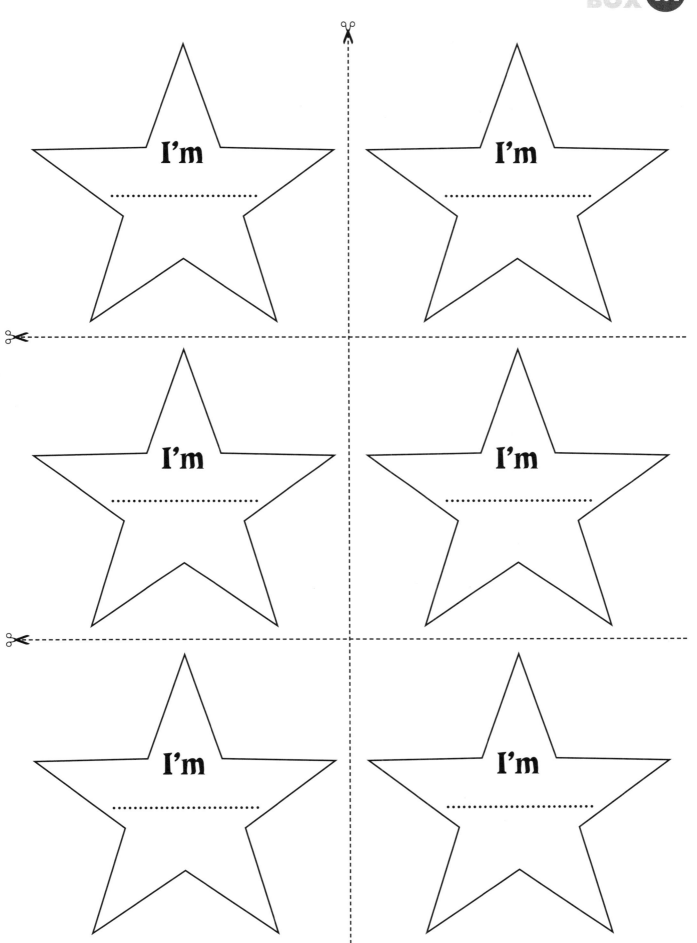

1.2

PRIMARY ACTIVITY BOX

All about me

ACTIVITY TYPE
individual form filling and
drawing

LANGUAGE FOCUS
language to talk about self,
physical appearance, age
and preferences:
I'm …
My hair is …
My eyes are …
My favourite … is …

LEVEL
2

AGE RANGE
9–11

SKILLS
reading, writing,
speaking (optional)

TIME
10–20 minutes

MATERIALS
a copy of the *All about me*
worksheet per pupil,
a tape measure or a wall
chart to measure pupils'
height

Before class
Make a photocopy of the *All about me* worksheet for each pupil.

In class
1 Revise the language used in the worksheet. Ask pupils questions to elicit the sentences on the sheet:
What's your name?   My name is Juanita.
Where are you from?   I'm from Málaga.

Do this for all the sentences, asking various pupils.

2 Give pupils a copy of the worksheet and ask them to complete the sentences. They then draw a picture of themselves in the frame. You can illustrate this with a picture of yourself inside a picture frame on the board.

3 When pupils have finished they can tell their partners about themselves.

Option
With confident pupils you can use this activity to practise question forms as pairwork. Practise the necessary question forms first. Give pupils the sheet and invite them to ask you questions to elicit the information on the sheet. You can write these questions on the board to help weaker pupils. Pupils then complete their own sheet and, when they have finished, ask their partners questions to find out what they have written.

Extension
As a follow-up to the option above, pupils could write the information their partner gives them on a separate worksheet such as the one below.

My friend's name is _____ .

He/She is from _____ .

He/She is _____ years old.

His/Her hair is _____ .

His/Her eyes are _____ .

He/She is _____ cm tall.

His/Her favourite colour is _____ .

His/Her favourite toy is _____ .

His/Her favourite animal is _____ .

My picture

My name is _____ .

I'm from _____ .

I'm _____ years old.

My hair is _____ .

My eyes are _____ .

I'm _____ cm tall.

My favourite colour is _____ .

My favourite toy is _____ .

My favourite animal is _____ .

My teacher's name is _____ .

My school is _____ .

1.3 My classroom friend

PRIMARY ACTIVITY BOX

ACTIVITY TYPE
individual reading
comprehension and drawing
activity

LANGUAGE FOCUS
parts of the body: *head, ears,
eyes, mouth, nose, body,
arms, legs, feet*
classroom objects: *rubber,
pencil sharpener, notebook,
pen, pencil, ruler*
shapes: *circle, square,
triangle*
colours

LEVEL
2

AGE RANGE
7–10

SKILLS
reading, listening (Extension)

TIME
10–20 minutes

MATERIALS
a copy of the *My classroom
friend* worksheet per pupil,
crayons

Before class

Make one copy of *My classroom friend* for each pupil.

In class

1 Check that pupils know the classroom vocabulary used in the text, by asking them to hold up objects. Say *Hold up your pencil, Hold up your ruler,* etc.

2 Give each pupil a copy of the worksheet.

3 On the board draw a frame for *My classroom friend*. Ask a pupil to read the first two sentences to you. Follow the instructions, and draw a *big pink rubber* (as a head) in the frame. Check that pupils understand that they must also draw a person following the description in the text.

4 If they are still not clear, continue and draw two pencil sharpeners for ears. Pupils should now be clear about how to complete the task.

5 Ask them to continue to read and draw their *classroom friend* in the frame. Circulate to monitor and help where needed.

6 When pupils have finished they can compare pictures with the pupils sitting near them.

Extension – 'Do This, Do That' game

This is a game to revise parts of the body.

1 Ask pupils to touch the different parts of their body. You may wish to concentrate on those used in the text or practise other parts of the body as well.
Touch your nose. Touch your mouth.

2 To make the game more challenging for pupils, ask them only to follow your instructions when you say *please*.
Touch your nose, please.   (Pupils touch their noses.)
Touch your nose.   (Pupils don't touch their noses.)

3 You can then play the game in a similar way to *Simon Says*. If you wish to make it competitive, those pupils who make a mistake are out and have to sit down.

4 The game can be extended by incorporating negative commands, and other vocabulary, e.g. *left* and *right*.

For more practice on parts of the body see **3.5 Body parts   5.2 Identikit**
For more practice on classroom vocabulary see **6.1 Whose is it?**

My classroom friend

Read and draw the picture.

This is my classroom friend.
His head is a big pink
rubber and his ears are two
small pencil sharpeners.
His eyes are big blue circles
and his mouth is a big red
square.
His nose is a small yellow
triangle.
His body is a yellow notebook.
His arms are two orange
pens and his legs are two
long blue rulers.
He's got two short green
pencils for feet.

MY CLASSROOM FRIEND

1.4

PRIMARY ACTIVITY BOX

Funometer

ACTIVITY TYPE
evaluation by pupils, giving feedback on a lesson or activity

LEVEL
1

AGE RANGE
5–10

TIME
5 minutes

MATERIALS
a copy of one assessment grid per pupil

This activity is intended to be used in conjunction with another task or activity. It is designed as an introduction to pupil evaluation of activities or lessons. The aim is to awaken pupils' interest in offering opinions about the kind of activities they like and/or dislike. It is a useful teaching/learning aid for both teachers and pupils.

Before class
Make enough photocopies and cut them up so that each pupil has an assessment grid. You can fill in the name or type of activity and/or the date before you make the photocopies so you have a clear record.

In class
1 After doing an activity give each pupil an assessment grid and explain the idea. The pupils circle the number to indicate their reaction to that activity or lesson and give the grid back to you. They do not need to write their names on it. You can create a feedback box if you want, (similar to those used in elections) where pupils can 'post' their pieces of paper.

2 You can then look at these pieces of paper to analyse the pupils' reactions and preferences. It is important to note here that you do not always have to do what the pupils want, but if you are aware of what pupils may not like, it is easier to pre-empt their dislike by explaining the value and positive side of any particular activity.

3 This kind of activity is best done on a regular basis so that pupils become accustomed to it. If you keep a record of pupils' reactions it is also a useful guide for future lesson planning.

Extension
Here is a different version of the grid, giving pupils the opportunity to say how easy or difficult they found an activity.

What you think	☺		☺		☹
	very easy	quite easy	OK	quite hard	very hard
Circle the number	5	4	3	2	1

What you think	☺		☺		☹
	very easy	quite easy	OK	quite hard	very hard
Circle the number	5	4	3	2	1

What you think	☺		☺		☹
	very easy	quite easy	OK	quite hard	very hard
Circle the number	5	4	3	2	1

What you think	☺		☺		☹
	very easy	quite easy	OK	quite hard	very hard
Circle the number	5	4	3	2	1

Funometer

Activity: _____

What you think	☺		☹		☹
	very good	good	OK	bad	very bad
Circle the number	5	4	3	2	1

Activity: _____

What you think	☺		☹		☹
	very good	good	OK	bad	very bad
Circle the number	5	4	3	2	1

Activity: _____

What you think	☺		☹		☹
	very good	good	OK	bad	very bad
Circle the number	5	4	3	2	1

Activity: _____

What you think	☺		☹		☹
	very good	good	OK	bad	very bad
Circle the number	5	4	3	2	1

Activity: _____

What you think	☺		☹		☹
	very good	good	OK	bad	very bad
Circle the number	5	4	3	2	1

Activity: _____

What you think	☺		☹		☹
	very good	good	OK	bad	very bad
Circle the number	5	4	3	2	1

Five star student

ACTIVITY TYPE:
teacher's assessment of
individual pupils'
performance or behaviour

LEVEL
1

AGE RANGE
6—11

TIME:
5 minutes

MATERIALS
a copy of one assessment
form per pupil

This activity serves as a complement to **1.4 Funometer**. Rather than lesson evaluation by pupils this is an introduction to pupil assessment by the teacher. You can interpret this assessment in terms of behaviour or performance along whatever lines are most suitable for your group. We have found it particularly useful for motivating pupils not to use their mother tongue in class. Other criteria might be: good behaviour in class, helpfulness, finishing an activity correctly and promptly, making an effort, consistency.

Before class
Make enough photocopies and cut them up so that each pupil has one form.

In class
1 Towards the end of the lesson give each pupil their form and ask them to complete their name and the date.

2 The teacher then assesses each pupil's performance and circles the number and star accordingly. Make it clear to your pupils that the assessment follows a standard scale from one to five depending on their performance, and make sure they are clear what it is they are being assessed on. If you wish, you could write it on the line at the top of the assessment form, e.g. 'Behaviour', 'Effort', 'For using English'.

3 Sign or initial the form.

4 Pupils can take their forms home to show their parents just how well they have done in class.

5 This can prove to be highly motivating if used on a regular basis, and helps to introduce pupils to the good-behaviour/reward concept at an early stage.

Five star student

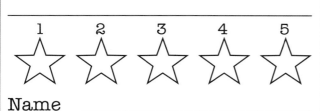

	1	2	3	4	5

Name _____

Date _____

Signed _____

	1	2	3	4	5

Name _____

Date _____

Signed _____

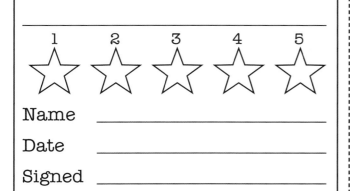

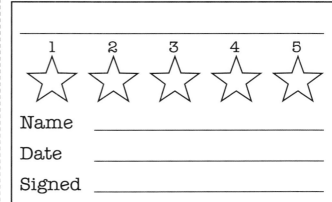

	1	2	3	4	5

Name _____

Date _____

Signed _____

	1	2	3	4	5

Name _____

Date _____

Signed _____

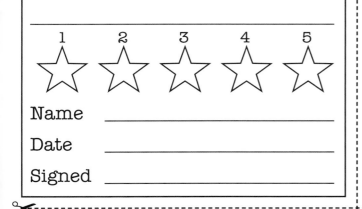

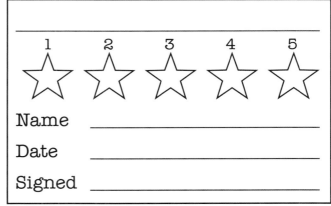

	1	2	3	4	5

Name _____

Date _____

Signed _____

	1	2	3	4	5

Name _____

Date _____

Signed _____

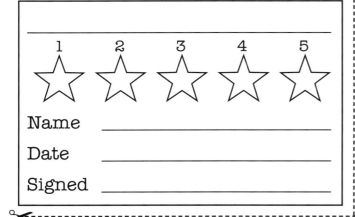

1.6

PRIMARY ACTIVITY BOX

Instructions dominoes

ACTIVITY TYPE
song, dominoes game played
in small groups as a matching
activity

LANGUAGE FOCUS
basic classroom instructions

LEVEL
2

AGE RANGE
6–9

SKILLS
reading

TIME
20–30 minutes

MATERIALS
a set of *Instructions dominoes*
per small group of pupils,
glue, scissors, cassette (for
song only)

Before class

Make one copy of the *Instructions dominoes* worksheet for each group of about four pupils and stick it onto card. Cut this up into 18 dominoes.

In class

1 Ensure that your pupils know the meaning of the words on the worksheet. You may want to revise them quickly or teach any they do not know.

2 As an introduction to some simple instructions, play the cassette or sing the song (to the tune of *Wind the Bobbin up*), demonstrating the actions at the same time.

Tapescript

Hold your pencil up.   (pupils hold up a pencil)
Hold your pencil up.
Write, draw, tap, tap, tap.   (pupils mime writing/drawing and tap their pencils on the desk)
Put it down again.   (pupils put the pencil down)
Put it down again.
Write, draw, tap, tap, tap.   (as before)
Point to the blackboard.   (pupils point as instructed)
Point to the floor.
Point to the window.
Point to the door.
Clap your hands together 1, 2, 3.
Now stand up and sing with me.

3 Practise the song line by line with your class, making sure that they repeat correctly and can do the actions.

4 When they are ready, pupils stand up and sing the whole song. When they have finished, pupils sit down ready to play the dominoes game.

5 Arrange the class in small groups working around a table.

6 Explain the rules. This can be done by example. Shuffle the dominoes and divide them between the pupils. Turn the last domino over and place it in the middle of the table.

7 The player to the left of the dealer starts. He or she puts a card next to the card on the table (either before or after). It must match the word or the picture. Encourage pupils to say the word as they put their dominoes down.

8 The player on his or her left continues and repeats the process. If any player cannot put a domino down then it is the next player's turn.

9 The first person to play all their dominoes is the winner. If no more dominoes can be put down at any point in the game, the winner is the player holding the least dominoes.

10 Monitor to check that the domino pairs are correct.

This is a good activity to use before any of the 'make and do' activities (see Section 8).

For another dominoes game see **6.2 Gramminoes**. There is also a *Dominoes* template on p.122 so that you can create your own version of a dominoes game.

Instructions dominoes

fold		stick		cut	
stand up		sit down		look	
listen		read		repeat	
write		sing		colour	
open		close	Shhh!	be quiet	
draw		point to	STOP	stop	

2.1

PRIMARY ACTIVITY BOX

Balloon game

ACTIVITY TYPE
individual 'listen and colour' activity

LANGUAGE FOCUS
colours: *red, green, blue, pink, yellow, orange, brown, purple, black, white, grey*
numbers 1 to 5
adjectives of size: *big, small, long*
Give me …

LEVEL
1

AGE RANGE
5–7

SKILLS
listening

TIME
15–30 minutes

MATERIALS
balloons (different colours and sizes), a copy of the *Balloon game* worksheet per pupil, crayons, cassette (optional)

Before class
Make a copy of the *Balloon game* worksheet for each pupil. Blow up different coloured balloons, including balloons of different sizes and shapes, if you wish.

In class
1 Bounce the balloons around the classroom.

2 Call children by their names, and ask them to bring you balloons, e.g. *Ian, give me the red balloon, please.*

3 You could make this into a game by dividing the class into teams and giving a point for bringing the correct balloon.

4 You can make the instructions more complex by using sizes as well (big, small, long), e.g. *Mary, give me the long, yellow balloon, please. Peter, give me the small, blue balloon, please.*

5 When all the balloons have been collected, give each pupil a copy of the worksheet and make sure they have their crayons ready. Play the cassette or read the tapescript, pausing to give pupils time to colour each balloon before moving on to the next one. As your pupils colour in, point out that new colours are made when two colours mix (where the balloons overlap).

Tapescript
Colour balloon number one red.
Colour balloon number two green.
Colour balloon number three blue.
Colour balloon number four pink.
Colour balloon number five yellow.

6 Teach pupils the names of the new colours (orange, brown and purple).

Extension
Call out two colours to elicit the new colour they make. Say:
red and yellow (orange)
blue and pink (purple)
yellow and blue (green)
black and white (grey)
red and green (brown)
red and white (pink)

Letter group

ACTIVITY TYPE
individual 'listen and colour' activity
pairwork follow-up

LANGUAGE FOCUS
letters of the alphabet whose names end in the same sound: *b, g, c, p, d, t, e, v*
colours
What colour is …?
It is …

LEVEL
1

AGE RANGE
6–9

SKILLS
listening, letter recognition, speaking

TIME
20–40 minutes

MATERIALS
a copy of the *Letter group* worksheet per pupil, crayons, cassette (optional)

Before class

Make a copy of the *Letter group* worksheet for each pupil.

In class

1 Revise the alphabet and its pronunciation. Focus especially on the letters on the worksheet and ask pupils what they have in common. (The names of the letters all end in the same sound – b (bee), c (cee), d (dee), etc.

2 Revise colours, using objects in the classroom and the question *What colour is …?*

3 Give pupils a copy each of the *Letter group* worksheet and make sure they have the necessary crayons.

4 Play the cassette or read the tapescript, pausing to give pupils time to colour each letter before moving on to the next one.

Tapescript

*Colour **b** brown.*
*Colour **g** green.*
*Colour **c** yellow.*
*Colour **p** purple.*
*Colour **d** orange.*
*Colour **t** grey.*
*Colour **e** blue.*
*Colour **v** red.*

5 Check that pupils have coloured the letters correctly by asking the question *What colour is **v**?* to elicit the answer *It is red*. Continue with the other letters.

6 Ask pupils to practise the question and answer form in pairs, and to ask about all the letters. They can use the question form above or even simplify it so that one pupil says the letter and the other pupil replies with the colour. If necessary illustrate by example. With more competent classes you can also introduce different question forms: *What/Which letter is red?* **V** *is.*

7 Similarly this can be used as an opportunity to practise yes/no question forms:
*Is **v** red? Yes, it is.*
*Is **b** blue? No, it isn't.*

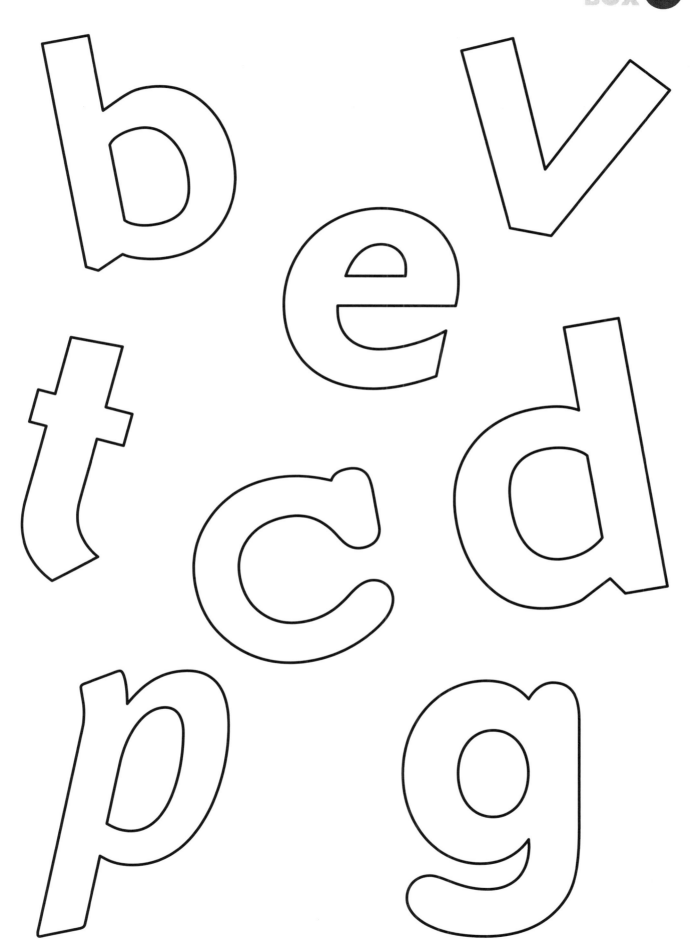

2.3 Join the alphadots

ACTIVITY TYPE
individual 'join the dots' activity

LANGUAGE FOCUS
letters of the alphabet
It is a(n) (elephant).

LEVEL
1

AGE RANGE
6–11

SKILLS
listening, letter recognition

TIME
20–30 minutes

MATERIALS
a copy of the *Join the alphadots* worksheet per pupil, crayons, cassette (optional)

Before class
Make a copy of the *Join the alphadots* worksheet for each pupil.

In class

1 Check your pupils' recognition of the letters of the alphabet. This can be done with a simple *Alphabet quiz*. The teacher says a word, e.g. *kite*, and the pupil has to say the first letter (k), to get a point. With more competent groups this can be extended to a *Spelling quiz*. The teacher asks pupils individually, in pairs or in teams, to spell simple words. They score one point for each correct word.

2 Give pupils a copy of the worksheet. Tell them to start by putting their pencils on the dot next to the pencil symbol. Ask them to listen to the cassette (or teacher) and draw the lines connecting the letters. Be prepared to pause the cassette if necessary.

Tapescript
p, d, x, v, t, r, j, b, h, k, l, o, u, q, s, g, f, a, i, n, e, c, y, p, m, z, w

3 Pupils then write the word under the picture:
It is an elephant.

Extension
Once your pupils have completed the name of the animal under the picture you can practise the structure *It is a/It is an* and the question form *Is it a/an …?* by playing a drawing game on the board.

Start by drawing the basic outline of something on the board. Pupils have to guess what it is by asking you questions, e.g. *Is it a book? Is it a box?* etc. To which you answer *Yes, it is./No, it isn't.* If necessary add details to the picture until they guess correctly what it is. (*It's a door!*)

When pupils understand how the game works let them come out to draw on the board. It is always a good idea for them to tell you what they are going to draw (or write it down) before they start, so as to save any discussion later.

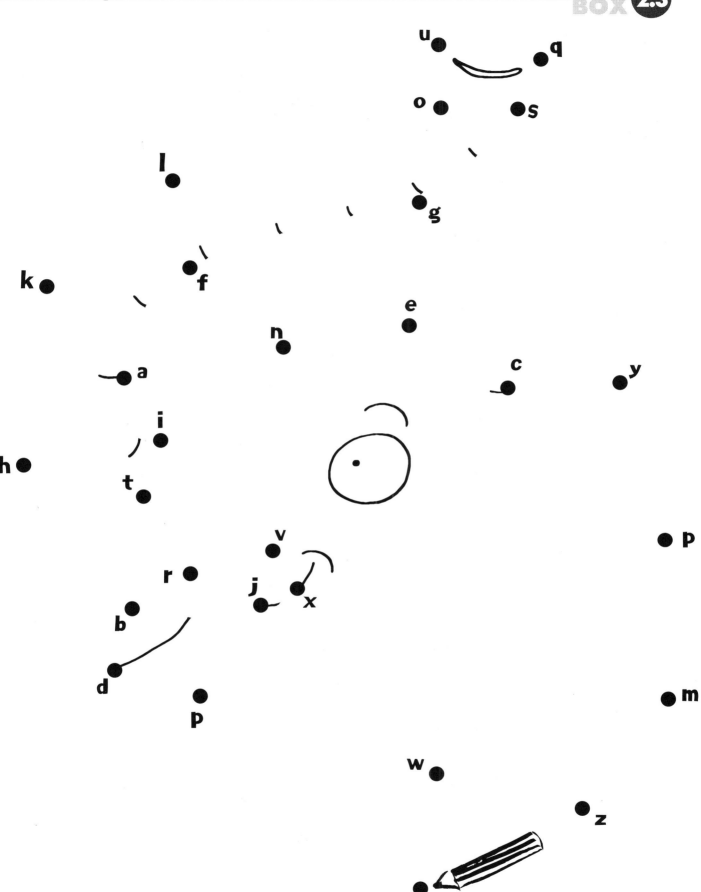

It is _____

PRIMARY ACTIVITY BOX

2.4 Join the dots

ACTIVITY TYPE
individual 'join the dots' activity, 'listen and colour', chant

LANGUAGE FOCUS
numbers 1–100
colours
clothes: *T-shirt, dress, trousers*

LEVEL
2

AGE RANGE
6–11

SKILLS
listening, speaking (Extension)

TIME
30–40 minutes

MATERIALS
a copy of the *Join the dots* worksheet per pupil, crayons, cassette (optional)

Before class
Make a copy of the *Join the dots* worksheet for each pupil.

In class
1 Check your pupils' recognition of the numbers 1–100. This can be done with a *Team blackboard race.*
  a Write a selection of numbers from 1–99 on the board.
  b Select two teams who line up, one behind the other, facing the board. Give the first member of each team a different coloured board pen or piece of chalk.
  c Read a number from the board, and the teams have to circle it. The first team to circle the number gets a point. The players in the team rotate so that everyone has a turn.

  This game is particularly useful for practising the problematical difference between thirty and thirteen, etc.

2 Give pupils a copy of the worksheet. Tell them to start by putting their pencils on the dot next to the pencil symbol. Ask them to listen to the cassette (or teacher) and draw the lines connecting the numbers. Be prepared to pause the cassette if necessary.

Tapescript – Listening 1

35, 27, 43, 76, 59, 24, 48, 31, 82, 17, 70, 13, 6, 18, 30, 63, 55, 78, 12, 15, 66, 92, 88, 94, 39, 42, 11.

3 Pupils then colour the picture with the following instructions:

Tapescript – Listening 2

Colour the T-shirt red. Colour the dog brown.
Colour the dress yellow. Colour the grass green.
Colour the trousers blue. Colour the flowers pink.

Extension – Washing line chant
Once pupils have finished the task you can teach them this chant to practise some of the vocabulary used in the lesson. Play the cassette or read the tapescript. Then practise it line by line with pupils. Finally they stand up and say the whole chant.

Tapescript – Listening 3

– What's the time?	– What's the time?	– What's the time?
– Half past nine.	– Half past nine.	– Half past nine.
– Hang your T-shirt on the line.	– Hang your dress on the line.	– Hang your trousers on the line.

Ask pupils to substitute more 'clothes' words.

For more practice on clothes see **5.6 Colour co-ordinates   6.5 Cowboy dot-to-dot 7.1 Jack and Jill   8.5 Dress me up**

2.5

ABC crossword

ACTIVITY TYPE
individual crossword, chant

LANGUAGE FOCUS
the alphabet and connected vocabulary

LEVEL
3

AGE RANGE
8–10

SKILLS
spelling (written and spoken)

TIME
50 minutes

MATERIALS
a copy of the *ABC crossword* worksheet per pupil, cassette (optional)

Before class

Make a copy of the *ABC crossword* worksheet for each pupil.

In class

1 Revise the alphabet and its pronunciation. If there is any vocabulary in the crossword that your class do not already know, make use of the illustrations to pre-teach it or, if you prefer, give them dictionaries to look the words up.

2 On the board draw a picture of an apple and a ball and this crossword grid.

3 Point to the picture of the apple and ask *What's this?* Look at the crossword on the board and ask your pupils *Where do I write it?* Ask them to spell it while you write it in the squares as they do so. Do the same for *ball*.

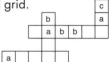

4 Give pupils a copy of the *ABC crossword* each. Ask them to look for a word which starts with the letter **c**, to put on the crossword on the board. When they say *cat* ask them to spell it and fill in the crossword, counting the number of letters and the number of boxes.

5 Ask them to continue like this and complete the crossword. Point out that each word starts with a different letter of the alphabet, and that there is a word for each letter of the alphabet. They should begin with words which already have a letter given, then those words will give them a letter for the next new word, etc. They should ignore the numbers on the crossword for the time being. These will be used when you correct the crossword together.

6 Circulate to help and prompt. Show pupils that the completed words on the crossword can also help them to solve the rest of the clues. As this puzzle requires a certain amount of reasoning give them plenty of time and if necessary push them in the right direction without giving them the answers.

7 Correct the crossword collectively. Individual pupils say the answers while you or other pupils write them on the board. The completed crossword is given on p. 126.

Option

To make the crossword easier, you could add some more letters before you photocopy.

Extension – Alphabet chant and game

To practise the alphabet, spelling and vocabulary play the *Alphabet chant* on cassette (or do it yourself with pupils). When the pupils chorus the letter, all click your fingers in unison.

Tapescript

TEACHER: Give me an A!	PUPILS: A!	TEACHER: Give me a B!	PUPILS: B!
TEACHER : Give me a P!	PUPILS: P!	TEACHER : Give me an A!	PUPILS: A!
TEACHER : Give me a P!	PUPILS: P!	TEACHER : Give me an L!	PUPILS: L!
TEACHER : Give me an L!	PUPILS: L!	TEACHER : Give me an L!	PUPILS: L!
TEACHER : Give me an E!	PUPILS: E!	TEACHER : What have you got?	PUPILS: Ball!
TEACHER : What have you got?	PUPILS: Apple!		

Now continue the chant as a game. The first pupil to put his/her hand up with the right answer to the question *What have you got?* wins a point. When pupils have got the idea, you could let some of them lead the chant (after first checking that they know the correct spelling of the word they have chosen).

ABC crossword

Rainy days

ACTIVITY TYPE
whole class rhyme, song and individual colour dictation

LANGUAGE FOCUS
colours
numbers 1–10

LEVEL
1

AGE RANGE
5–7

SKILLS
saying a rhyme, listening

TIME
30 minutes

MATERIALS
a copy of the *Rainy days* worksheet per pupil, crayons, cassette (optional)

Before class

Make a copy of the *Rainy days* worksheet for each pupil.

In class

1 Give pupils a worksheet each and pre-teach *rain* and *raindrops*.

2 Play the cassette or read the tapescript.

Tapescript – Listening 1

Rain, rain go away.
Come again another day.

3 Practise the rhyme line by line with the class. Then say it together.

4 Next play the song on cassette or sing it to the class. (It also works well as a rhyme.)

Tapescript – Listening 2

I hear thunder.	(Hold your right hand to your right ear.)
I hear thunder.	(Hold your right hand to your right ear.)
Oh! Don't you?	(Signal to the person in front of you with hands in a questioning way.)
Oh! Don't you?	(Signal to the person in front of you with hands in a questioning way.)
Pitter patter raindrops.	(Hold your hands out, palms down, and drum the air with your fingers.)
Pitter patter raindrops.	(Hold your hands out, palms down, and drum the air with your fingers.)
I'm wet through.	(Hug yourself and shiver.)
So are you.	(Signal to the person in front of you with your hands.)

5 Practise the song line by line with your class, making sure that they repeat correctly and can do the actions. When they are ready sing the song together, doing the actions.

6 Ask pupils to turn to their worksheets and colour them according to the instructions they are about to hear. Play the cassette or read the tapescript, pausing to give pupils time to colour each section before moving on to the next one.

Tapescript – Listening 3

Colour number nine blue. Colour number three green.
Colour number one yellow. Colour number six pink.
Colour number seven orange. Colour number eight brown.
Colour number four purple. Colour number five red.
Colour number ten grey. Colour number two black.

7 When they have finished colouring, check with the whole class that they have done the activity correctly by asking questions such as *What colour is number 5?* (Red.)

For another rainy day activity see **7.2 Incy Wincy Spider**
For more practice on numbers 1–10 see **7.4 My fish tank**

Rain rhymes

2.7

My alphabet book

ACTIVITY TYPE
individual 'make and do' activity, song

LANGUAGE FOCUS
letters of the alphabet, basic vocabulary

LEVEL
2

AGE RANGE
6–9

SKILLS
listening, writing

TIME
40–50 minutes

MATERIALS
a copy of the *My alphabet book* worksheet (both sides) per pupil, crayons, pictures from magazines (optional), scissors, glue, cassette (optional)

Before class
Make a double-sided photocopy of *My alphabet book*. If you can't do this, then stick the two pages together (back-to-back).

In class
1 Check your pupils' recognition of the letters of the alphabet or revise them using the alphabet song. Play the cassette or sing the song from the tapescript.

2 Practise the song line by line with the class. When they are ready, ask them to stand up and sing the whole song.

Tapescript
A B C D E F G
H I J K L M N O P
Q R S and T U V
W X and Y and Z.
Now you know your ABC
Can you sing along with me?

3 On the board draw an apple. Say *A is for …?* to elicit *A is for apple*. Write this next to the picture of the apple.

4 Say *B is for …?* and wait for suggestions (*banana, ball, blackboard, bag, etc.*). Choose one of these, draw a quick picture and write *B is for …* (depending on the word chosen).

5 Give pupils their copy of the photocopied sheet. Show them how to fold it so that it has the form of a booklet and ask them to fold their own.

6 Now ask them to write their names and to proceed by drawing pictures for words which start with each letter of the alphabet, and writing the short text next to each picture.

Options
a Pupils can cut pictures out of magazines and stick them next to the words.
b Pupils can list all the words they know beginning with each letter.

Extension: – 'One, two, three' class game
Select a theme, e.g. 'words beginning with B'. Tap the table twice saying 'one, two', then click your fingers saying 'three', then say the word, e.g. 'one, two, three – ball'. The pupils then have to continue, in turn, saying different words. If pupils repeat a word or take longer than ten seconds, they are out.

Alphabet tennis – pairwork
A pupil says a letter to his or her partner. The partner says a word beginning with that letter. The first pupil says another word beginning with the same letter, and they continue in this way until one of them runs out of words.

My Alphabet Book

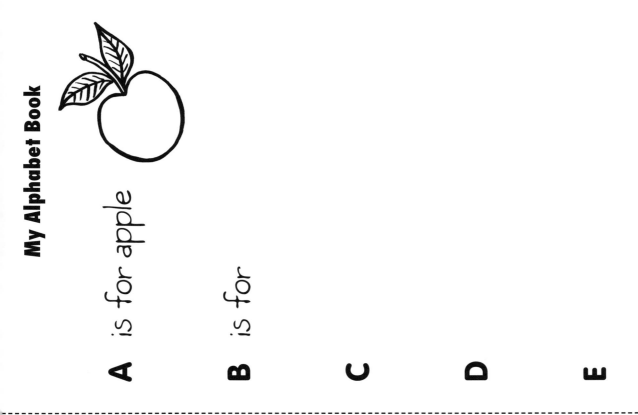

A is for apple

B is for

C

D

E

- -

Fold here

T

U

V

W

X

Y

Z

M   N   O   P   Q   R   S

- -

F   G   H   I   J   K   L

 From *Primary Activity Box* by C. Nixon and M. Tomlinson © Cambridge University Press 2001

PRIMARY ACTIVITY BOX 3.1

Card games

ACTIVITY TYPE
whole class and small group
card games: *Pelmanism* and
Snap! (matching activities)

LANGUAGE FOCUS
either *animal* or *food and
drink* vocabulary
game-playing vocabulary:
Whose turn is it?
It's my turn.
*How many pairs have you
got?*

LEVEL
1

AGE RANGE
5–8

SKILLS
word recognition, speaking

TIME
20 minutes per game

MATERIALS
copies of either the *Animal* or
Food and drink card sets,
card, scissors, crayons, glue

Before class

Decide which set of vocabulary you want to practise (*Animals* or *Food and drink*) and make photocopies of the appropriate set of cards.

For **Pelmanism** you will need **one set** of cards per group of four pupils.
For **Snap!** you will need **two sets** of cards per pair or group of pupils.

Colour the pictures and, if possible, stick the photocopies onto stiff card (so that the pictures cannot be seen through the paper) before you cut them up into individual playing cards. If your pupils are old enough, they can make their own sets of cards in class and colour them.

In class

Pelmanism

1 The game can be played first as a whole class team game and then in groups of four.

2 Demonstrate the game to the class with a group of four pupils. Using a big table or the floor, spread the cards out, face down.

3 In turn, pupils turn over two cards at a time to find a matching pair (picture and name, or picture and picture depending on the age of your pupils – see Note below).

4 If the two upturned cards do not match, the pupil turns them face down again in their original position and the next pupil continues in the same way. When pupils find a pair they must say the sentence *It's ...* and then they can keep the pair of cards.

5 They continue until no cards are left on the table. The winner is the pupil with the most pairs.

6 Circulate as they play. Encourage pupils to use English for communicating while they play by teaching them some essential phrases beforehand, e.g. *Whose turn is it? It's my turn. How many pairs have you got? You're the winner.*

Note

This game can be played with a picture/picture mix for very young learners, in which case you need to photocopy two sets of picture cards per group.

Snap!

1 Snap can be played in small groups (maximum four pupils) or pairs.

2 Demonstrate the game by example with one of your pupils.

3 Take the sets of cards, shuffle them and deal the cards all out between the two of you. You both keep your pile of cards face down on the table.

4 Start by taking the first card off your pack, turn it over face up and put it in the centre of the table. Your partner does the same, putting the card on top of yours. If the cards match (picture + picture, word + word or word + picture), the first person to say *Snap!* takes the pile of cards and puts them to the bottom of their own pile. If the two cards are different, you continue by turning over cards in turn and putting them down as before. The game is over when one person has all the cards (they are the winner).

5 Encourage pupils to use English for communicating while they play by teaching them some essential phrases beforehand: *It's my turn. Whose turn is it?* Circulate as they play. With any game that includes an element of competition children can get excited and noisy.

For more practice on animals see **8.1 Farmyard fun**

39

giraffe		zebra	
hippo		seal	
rhino		penguin	
tiger		snake	
lion		elephant	

 From *Primary Activity Box* by C. Nixon and M. Tomlinson © Cambridge University Press 2001

Card games: Food and drink set

PRIMARY ACTIVITY BOX 3.1

eggs		cake	
orange juice		ice cream	
milk		fruit	
lemonade		cheese	
water		meat	

From *Primary Activity Box* by C. Nixon and M. Tomlinson © Cambridge University Press 2001 PHOTOCOPIABLE 41

PRIMARY ACTIVITY
BOX

What are they doing?

ACTIVITY TYPE
individual crossword

LANGUAGE FOCUS
present continuous
basic verbs of action: *write,
draw, watch, ride, dance,
eat, read, listen, run, wash,
drink*

LEVEL
2

AGE RANGE
8–11

SKILLS
writing, speaking (Extension)

TIME
20–40 minutes

MATERIALS
a copy of the *What are they
doing?* worksheet per pupil

Before class
Make a copy of the *What are they doing?* worksheet for each pupil.

In class

1 Draw a horizontal arrow on the board and write *Across*. Draw a vertical arrow on the board and write *Down*.

2 Draw the following on the board:

3 Mime or draw the action *writing* and ask *What am I doing?* to elicit *You are writing*.

4 Say *Can you spell 'writing'?* and write it in the squares on the board as your pupils dictate it to you.

5 Give a copy of the worksheet to each of your pupils.

6 Direct them to the picture of 2 across and ask *What is he doing?* to elicit *He's writing*. Point to 2 across in the crossword and tell them to put *writing* in the squares.

7 Tell them also to write *He's writing.* on the lines next to the picture.

8 Tell them to continue in the same way for the other pictures. Make sure they use the correct subject pronoun and have the correct verb agreement.

9 Circulate to monitor and help.

10 Once they have finished, correct the crossword orally: one pupil asks the question (*What is he doing?*) and another pupil answers (*He is reading.*) etc. Check they have used the correct spelling by asking one pupil to spell the word while you, or another pupil, writes it on the board.

Key

Across
  4 She's drawing
  7 They're watching
10 She's riding
11 They're dancing

Down
  1 She's listening
  3 They're running
  5 He's washing
  6 He's eating
  8 She's drinking
  9 She's reading

Option
Pupils can make their own crosswords, using the *DIY wordsearch* photocopy on p. 113 as a base.

Extension – Mime game

1 Illustrate by example. Mime an action, and ask pupils *What am I doing?* Pupils answer *You are* (*watching television, reading*, etc.).

2 Ask individual pupils to come out and mime actions (and ask the question) for the other members of the class to guess. Alternatively you could prepare cue cards with verbs and ask the pupil to take a card and mime the action on the card.

For more practice on the present continuous see **6.5 Cowboy dot-to-dot**
For another crossword see **2.5 ABC crossword**

What are they doing?

Across

2 _____ _____ .

4 _____ _____
a picture.

7 _____ _____ television.

10 _____ _____
a bike.

11 _____ _____ .

6 _____ _____ a sandwich.

Down

1 _____ _____ to the radio.

3 _____ _____ .

5 _____ _____
the dishes.

8 _____ _____ .

9 _____ _____
a book.

3.3

PRIMARY ACTIVITY BOX

Mix 'n' match

ACTIVITY TYPE

matching activity, to be done in pairs

LANGUAGE FOCUS

combination of verb + noun or particle
revision of any verb tense

LEVEL

3

AGE RANGE

9–11

SKILLS

reading, writing (optional)

TIME

45 minutes

MATERIALS

a copy of the Mix 'n' match worksheet per pair of pupils

Before class

Make a copy of the *Mix 'n' match* worksheet for each pair or small group of pupils. If possible, stick the worksheet onto card before you cut it up, to make the word cards easier to handle for pupils. Check if there are any words or phrases which you do not want to include, and, if so, discard them. Cut up the worksheet into 66 cards.

In class

1 Arrange the class into pairs and give each pair a set of word cards.

2 Explain the object of the activity. This can be done by example on the blackboard. Write a verb on one side of the board and a number of possible combinations on the other, e.g.

	a sandwich
	a letter
	up
watch	television
	a photo
	a car

Elicit the correct combination from pupils: *watch television*.

3 Ask the pairs of pupils to match up their cards in the same way.

4 Monitor to check that they are making correct combinations. NB There is sometimes more than one correct combination, e.g. *open a letter* would be correct, as well as *open the door*.

Optional written work

1 When they have completed the task, ask pupils to write sentences using some of the combinations they have created. These can be made using any tense they have been working on recently, e.g.
I am watching the television.
Sarah never watches television.

2 Put pupils into teams and ask pupils in each team in turn to read out a sentence.

3 Teams score a point for each correct sentence.

Option

Select the combinations you want to use with your class and write the words on large pieces of card. Give one card to each pupil, then ask pupils to walk around to find their other half. For example, the pupil with the card *watch* walks around until she finds *television*. When all the pupils have found their partner they can make up sentences in pairs using their words. These can then be read out to the whole class in a team game, as above, if you like.

your hair	brush	television	watch	a picture	draw
your teeth	clean	jeans	wear	a sandwich	eat
your face	wash	lemonade	drink	tennis	play
homework	do your	a bike	ride	a car	drive
a book	read	a letter	write	quiet	be
the flowers	pick	a photo	take	a kite	fly
'hello'	say	French	speak	to ten	count
up	stand	down	sit	the radio	listen to
in Africa	live	the door	open	a lesson	have
the key	forget	a ticket	buy	the lions	feed
swimming	go	a ladder	climb	a song	sing

3.4 PRIMARY ACTIVITY BOX
Colourful cans

ACTIVITY TYPE
preposition practice with hand movements
individual 'listen and colour' activity

LANGUAGE FOCUS
colours
prepositions of place: *next to, under, between*
numbers 1–9

OPTION
on the left/right of, above, below, beside

LEVEL
2

AGE RANGE
6–9

SKILLS
listening

TIME
20–30 minutes

MATERIALS
a copy of the *Colourful cans* worksheet per pupil, crayons, cassette (optional)

Before class

Make a copy of the *Colourful cans* worksheet for each pupil.

In class

1 Revise the prepositions in class using your hands as follows.
   Use your left hand as the base and with your right hand illustrate the following:
   next to   Place your flat right hand next to your clenched left hand.
   between   Place your flat right hand between the second and third fingers of your left hand.
   under   Place your flat right hand under your clenched left hand.

2 Ask your pupils to stand up and place their hands in the right position according to your instructions: *under, next to* or *between*.

3 Give your pupils a copy of *Colourful cans*. Tell them to listen and colour the cans according to the instructions.

4 Play the cassette or read the tapescript. You may need to pause the cassette or repeat it several times.

Tapescript – Listening 1

Colour can number one <u>brown</u>. Colour the can under number six <u>red</u>.
Colour the can between four and six <u>yellow</u>. Colour the can next to number three <u>purple</u>.
Colour the can under number four <u>orange</u>. Colour the can between number one and number seven <u>pink</u>.
Colour the can under number three <u>grey</u>. Colour the can between numbers seven and nine <u>blue</u>.
The can next to the purple can is <u>green</u>.

5 Correct the activity orally. Pupils tell you what colour each can is: *Can number nine is red,* etc.

Key

The cans are coloured as follows in both the original exercise and the Option:
1 – brown 2 – purple 3 – green 4 – pink 5 – yellow 6 – grey 7 – orange 8 – blue 9 – red.

Option

1 As an alternative you may prefer to make the dictation more complicated, incorporating other prepositional phrases, such as *on the left of, on the right of, below, above* and *beside*.

2 Ask three pupils to stand up and come to the front of the class. Use the following commands: *Stand on the left of Peter. Stand on the right of Jane. Stand between Jane and Andrew.* and make sure they position themselves accordingly.

3 Play the cassette or read the tapescript. Pupils listen and colour the cans.

Tapescript – Listening 2

Colour the can in the middle <u>yellow</u>. Colour the can on the left of number two <u>brown</u>.
Colour the can beside number three <u>purple</u>. Colour the can below number four <u>orange</u>.
Colour the can on the right of number eight <u>red</u>. Colour the can between numbers seven and nine <u>blue</u>.
Colour the can above number seven <u>pink</u>. The can on the right of the purple can is <u>green</u>.
The can above the red can is <u>grey</u>.

For more practice on prepositions see **5.4 Room for improvement 9.5 Shaping up**

3.5

Body parts

ACTIVITY TYPE
pairwork: vocabulary
matching exercise, song

LANGUAGE FOCUS
parts of the body
left, right

LEVEL
2

AGE RANGE
7–10

SKILLS
singing, reading, listening
(Extension)

TIME
30–45 minutes

MATERIALS
a copy of the *Body parts*
worksheet per pupil, sticky
tape, scissors, cassette
(optional)

Before class

Make a copy of the *Body parts* worksheet for each pupil and cut it into 20 cards. Older pupils can cut up their own cards.

In class

1 Using the cassette or tapescript, get pupils to listen to the song and then repeat it, first line by line and then completely. Then repeat it with the actions. Pupils must touch each particular part of their body as they sing the word. When they repeat the song the second time they touch their head but they do not say the word. When they repeat it the third time, they miss out the words *head* and *shoulders*; the fourth time they miss out *head, shoulders* and *knees*, etc. They continue until they touch all the parts in sequence without saying any of the words. Then sing the whole song again faster and faster.

Tapescript

Head, shoulders, knees and toes, knees and toes
Head, shoulders, knees and toes, knees and toes
And eyes and ears and mouth and nose
Head, shoulders, knees and toes, knees and toes.

2 Practise *left* and *right* (see Extension). Arrange your class in pairs. Give each pupil a set of cards or a copy of the worksheet which they have to cut into cards.

3 In each pair, one pupil acts as a model while the other pupil labels the appropriate parts of the model's body using the cards and sticky tape. For the eyes, they should stick the labels on the forehead, with the arrows pointing down towards the eye.

4 Circulate to monitor and help.

5 Pupils change roles. When they have finished they walk around the classroom comparing other pupils' labels and help each other correct them if necessary.

Extension

One pupil comes to the front of the class and another pupil or teacher gives 'orders', e.g. *Touch your right eye. Touch your left shoulder,* etc. Or, it can be done collectively as a class, eliminating those that carry out the order incorrectly by asking them to sit down.

Note

Ask pupils to be careful when they stick their labels on their partners!

For more practice on parts of the body/physical description see **5.2 Identikit**
5.5 You read, I write

48

head	hair	nose	mouth
hand	left foot	left knee	left leg
toes	right foot	right knee	right leg
left ear	left eye ⬇	left arm	left shoulder
right ear	right eye ⬇	right arm	right shoulder

Timescales

Before class
Make a photocopy of *Timescales* per pupil, pair or small group and cut up into cards. Keep each set of cards separate.

In class
1 Give each pupil, pair or group of pupils a set of cards and ask them to spread the cards out on the desk before them. Let them look at them for a few minutes to familiarise themselves with their contents.

2 Explain by example. Draw a few matching cards on the board with different times and sentences from those in the pupils' sets. Explain that the activity consists of matching the sentences with the digital clock.

3 Circulate to monitor and correct.

4 When pupils have finished matching the pairs correctly, ask them to make a 'ladder' with the first action/time at the top and the last one at the bottom, thus putting the daily routine in chronological order.

Optional written work
With more competent groups ask them to write about their own day in the same way.

Extension
Arrange pupils in groups of four to six and ask them to find the answers to the following questions in their group.

Who gets up first?	_____
Who gets home first?	_____
Who finishes their homework first?	_____
Who has dinner last?	_____
Who goes to bed last?	_____

Before they begin, make sure they understand *first* and *last*. Check that they know what questions to ask, i.e. *What time do you ...?*

11:40	She has a maths lesson at twenty to twelve.
10:20	At twenty past ten she has an English lesson.
8:45	She eats her breakfast at quarter to nine.
9:15	She arrives at school at quarter past nine.
1:05	At five past one she eats her lunch at school.
12:55	Her lessons finish at five to one.
7:15	She watches television at quarter past seven.
6:30	She does her homework at half past six.
4:25	She plays in the park at twenty-five past four.
3:35	She goes home at twenty-five to four.
7:50	She gets up at ten to eight.
11:10	She plays with her friends at ten past eleven.
8:10	She has a shower at ten past eight.
9:00	She leaves home at nine o'clock.
5:30	She has dinner at half past five.

3.7

PRIMARY ACTIVITY BOX

Word scramble

ACTIVITY TYPE
group vocabulary and
spelling game

LANGUAGE FOCUS
letters
simple vocabulary

LEVEL
2

AGE RANGE
8–11

SKILLS
word production, spelling

TIME
30 minutes

MATERIALS
one copy of the *Word
scramble* worksheet per pair
or group of 3–4 pupils

Before class

Make a copy of the *Word scramble* worksheet for each pair or group of 3–4 pupils. Cut each copy up into individual letter cards.

In class

1 This game can be played in pairs or small groups (maximum four pupils).

2 Before giving out the letter cards, demonstrate the game by example with a group at the front of the classroom.
  – Place the letters face down on the table.
  – Each player takes twelve letters and places them face up on the table in front of them. They then have five minutes to make as many words as they can using their selection of letters, writing these words on a separate piece of paper. They can use only the letters they have per word, but they can re-use them for the next word.
  – Words can be scored according to the number of letters they contain: a point for each letter as in the example:

| b | c | e | g | t | l | c | a | h | k | p | y | o |

boat ✓ 4 points   cake ✓ 4 points
coat ✓ 4 points   tall ✗ 0 points
bat ✓ 3 points   (*tall* isn't possible because there is only one 'l' in the selection)
back ✓ 4 points

  – For the demonstration game the teacher helps pupils with scoring, but they should then be able to score their own words.
  – If you want your pupils to play more rounds of the game, then they should mix the letters face down on the table again and select another twelve.

3 Give each group their cards and let them play.

4 Circulate to monitor and help.

Option

As spelling practice, you can say a word and each group spells it with their letters.
Ask individual pupils to write the words on the board for correction.

For more practice on word formation see **9.1 DIY wordsearch**

a	a	a	a	a	a	a	a	b
b	c	c	d	d	d	d	e	e
e	e	e	e	e	e	e	e	e
f	f	g	g	g	h	h	i	i
i	i	i	i	i	i	j	k	k
l	l	l	l	m	m	m	n	n
n	n	n	n	o	o	o	o	o
o	o	o	p	p	p	q	r	r
r	r	r	r	s	s	s	s	t
t	t	t	t	t	u	u	u	u
v	v	v	w	w	x	x	y	y	z

3.8

PRIMARY ACTIVITY BOX

Three in a line

ACTIVITY TYPE
individual, pair or small
group vocabulary activity

LANGUAGE FOCUS
different lexical groups

LEVEL
3

AGE RANGE
8–11

SKILLS
reading

TIME
30 minutes

MATERIALS
a copy of the *Three in a line*
worksheet per pupil, pair or
small group

Before class

Make a copy of the *Three in a line* worksheet for each pupil, pair or small group. As a shorter activity, you can photocopy a smaller section of the worksheet.

In class

1 Draw four large circles on the board. Title them *Clothes, Animals, Toys* and *Food*.

2 Ask the class to give examples of vocabulary for each lexical group. Write them in the circles.

3 In the circle titled *Clothes* write *sandwich* at the bottom of the list. Ask *Is this correct?* and *Where does 'sandwich' go?* to elicit the correct response.

4 Draw the following example on the board.

cat	shoe	ruler
dog	pen	table
pencil	sock	trousers

5 Choose a line of words (horizontal, vertical or diagonal) from the grid that are not in the same lexical group and say, for example: *Cat, dog, pencil – is that right?*

6 Repeat the same procedure with another three words.

7 Repeat the procedure with the three words from the same lexical group (*pencil, pen, ruler*) and draw a line through the words. If your pupils were not able to see the connection, repeat the explanation with another example.

8 Give your pupils the worksheet. Ask them to do the exercise. Tell them the lines can be horizontal, vertical or diagonal.

9 Correct collectively. Ask pupils to justify their answers to encourage discussion. Ask them if they can give each completed grid a suitable title (e.g. Clothes, Pets, Vehicles, etc.).

Key

1 kite – skateboard – ball
2 book – comic – magazine
3 grass – tree – flower
4 dog – cat – hamster
5 school – hospital – museum
6 tea – coffee – milk
7 history – science – maths
8 apple – banana – lemon
9 mother – father – brother
10 bus – car – lorry
11 shoe – sock – boot
12 kitchen – bathroom – bedroom

Option

With more competent pupils you can ask them to make up their own grids which they can give other pupils to do. You may want to select the best of these and photocopy them for later use.

Extension

Choose five lexical groups and write a different word from each group onto cards (one word per card). Make enough cards for each pupil in the class. Give pupils a card each and ask them to move around the class finding the other members of their lexical group.

Three in a line

1

kite	racket	sweater
skateboard	jeans	computer game
ball	shoe	balloon

2

newspaper	book	pen
cassette	comic	sweets
compact disc	magazine	box

3

insect	girl	plant
grass	tree	flower
dog	bird	boy

4

dog	tiger	canary
elephant	cat	giraffe
hippo	mouse	hamster

5

school	street	bus stop
library	hospital	park
car	bus	museum

6

bread	tea	kitchen
cola	coffee	butter
water	milk	cheese

7

school	classroom	maths
French	science	teacher
history	geography	student

8

tea	chicken	hamburger
ice-cream	milk	meat
apple	banana	lemon

9

mother	grandfather	doctor
father	friend	grandmother
brother	sister	teacher

10

port	taxi	lorry
airport	car	station
bus	sea	boat

11

shoe	dress	bed
sock	chair	hat
boot	book	trousers

12

stairs	window	kitchen
fridge	dining room	bathroom
garden	door	bedroom

55

Legs! Legs! Legs!

ACTIVITY TYPE
individual pronunciation and
reading puzzle

LANGUAGE FOCUS
basic vocabulary and its
pronunciation (/e/ and /iː/)

LEVEL
3

AGE RANGE
9–11

SKILLS
listening, reading and
distinguishing sounds /e/
and /iː/

TIME
20–40 minutes

MATERIALS
a copy of the *Legs! Legs!
Legs!* worksheet per pupil

Before class

Make a copy of the *Legs! Legs! Legs!* worksheet for each pupil.

In class

1 Stand in front of the class and say, '*Look and listen*'. Raise your leg quickly (marching soldier style) and say *leg*. Stress the target sound /e/. Bend your knees slowly and say *kneeees*, exaggerating the sound and drawing it out in time with the knee bend. In this way you effectively stress the target sound /iː/ and your pupils have a visual image of the two different sounds, long (/iː/) and short (/e/).

2 Say *Listen and repeat: leg, knee, leg, knee* alternately raising your leg and bending your knees. Ask the class to repeat the actions with you several times as they say the words.

3 Say *Green – knee or leg?* Wait for the class to discover the similarity between the sounds and to offer an answer. If the answer is correct say, *Good. Green – knee*, stressing the target sound /iː/ and accompanying it with the action. If the answer is incorrect say, *Green – leg? Or Green – knee?*, whilst carrying out the actions. Stress and contrast the target sounds so that your pupils can hear the difference.

4 Repeat the process with other words containing the target sounds from the following lists:
knee, green, three, he, me, tree, bee, feet, teeth, cheese, jeans, week, queen, she, tea, key, clean, meat, street, between
leg, red, ten, hen, desk, pen, pencil, yes, seven, bed, egg, red, head, left, friend, breakfast, empty, heavy, leopard, weather, wet, twelve, question

Ask pupils to stand up and respond to each prompt with the corresponding action.

5 Give out the worksheet and demonstrate the activity to the class. Explain that pupils must draw lines through the words with the 'leg' vowel sound /e/ starting at the start arrow and finishing at the finish arrow. Insist that they use pencil so that they can rub out and correct as they go along. Demonstrate the first three words (leg, letter, pen).

6 Point out to pupils that they can go left, right, up or down but *not* diagonally. They may have to go back on themselves, so they must look at all the words.

7 Circulate to monitor, prompt and help.

8 Correct the exercise orally.

Key

Pupils must follow this route:
leg – letter – pen – seven – yes – elephant – twelve – head – pencil – desk – penguin – ten – egg – tennis – zebra – bed – dress – lemon – question – hen – teddy

Extension – Team game

1 Write two different sets of *knee* and *leg* words (see the lists above) on sheets of paper.

2 Draw a line down the centre of the board and write A and B at the top of each half. Below each letter write the words *leg* and *knee* to form two columns on each side of the board.

3 Divide the class into two teams A and B, and give each team a set of the words. Set a time limit for the teams to stick or write the words in the correct column on the board. The team with the most correct answers wins.

Legs! Legs! Legs!

Follow the 'leg' words.

start						
leg	letter	tree	head	pencil	desk	hand
cat	pen	eight	twelve	car	penguin	lion
dog	seven	yes	elephant	knee	ten	bear
tiger	feet	ear	snake	tennis	egg	orange
leopard	sweater	ruler	eye	zebra	jeans	rubber
key	leaf	book	shirt	bed	feet	cheese
shorts	cake	skirt	sea	dress	lemon	mouse
pie	bike	sock	arm	water	question	hen
						finish

4.2 Rhyming words

ACTIVITY TYPE
individual pronunciation activity

LANGUAGE FOCUS
pronunciation of simple vocabulary

LEVEL
2

AGE RANGE
7–10

SKILLS
pronunciation, writing

TIME
40–50 minutes

MATERIALS
a copy of the *Rhyming words* worksheet per pupil

Before class
Make a copy of the *Rhyming words* worksheet for each pupil. As a shorter activity, you can photocopy a smaller section of the worksheet.

In class
1 Revise or pre-teach vocabulary from the worksheet.
2 Draw a picture of a cat and a hat on the blackboard. Write *cat* and *hat* next to the pictures.
3 Say *Listen and repeat. Cat, hat.* Wait for your class to repeat. Correct pronunciation if necessary.
4 Write *yes* and *no* next to the pictures, and ask *cat, hat – Do they rhyme?* When your class have responded, draw a circle around *yes.*
5 Repeat the procedure for two words that do not rhyme. They do not necessarily have to appear on the worksheet.
6 Give pupils the worksheet and ask them to continue in the same way.
7 Circulate to monitor and help.
8 Correct collectively, pupils pronouncing the two words correctly before giving you the answer.

Key

1 house – horse no	8 bed – bread yes	15 tree – three yes
2 sun – one yes	9 star – car yes	16 book – foot no
3 skirt – kite no	10 flower – four no	17 sock – clock yes
4 foot – goat no	11 dog – clock no	18 sun – moon no
5 four – door yes	12 shirt – skirt yes	19 mouse – house yes
6 box – book no	13 wall – ball yes	20 shoe – two yes
7 plane – train yes	14 moon – one no	

Non-readers
If your pupils are non-readers or weaker at reading you may wish to omit the written part of the activity.

Extension
Write some of the following sentences on the board. Pupils must circle the words that rhyme.

1 There's a small ball near the wall.
2 The boys are playing with toys.
3 The girls are wearing skirts and shirts.
4 There's some fish in the dish.
5 The old goat is eating a coat.
6 There's a mouse in the house.
7 There's a fox between the rocks.
8 The man is under the van.
9 There's a frog on the log.
10 The children like their bike.
11 That bear has got long, brown hair.
12 There's a fat cat sitting on the mat.
13 He's got a new, blue shoe.
14 Ten men have got a red hen.
15 The frog is between the log and the dog.
16 She's got a white kite in her right hand.
17 He's got a cold nose and toes when it snows.
18 What can we do? We can go to the zoo.
19 Where is my teddy bear? It's there on the chair.
20 Jack has got a black sack on his back.
21 We can't see our kite at night when it isn't light.
22 I've got six blue bricks and two drum sticks.

More proficient pupils can try to invent their own sentences like those above.

Rhyming words

Example (yes)

cat

hat

no

7 yes ___ no

14 yes ___ no

1 yes ___ no

8 yes ___ no

15 yes ___ no

2 yes ___ no

9 yes ___ no

16 yes ___ no

3 yes ___ no

10 yes ___ no

17 yes ___ no

4 yes ___ no

11 yes ___ no

18 yes ___ no

5 yes ___ no

12 yes ___ no

19 yes ___ no

6 yes ___ no

13 yes ___ no

20 yes ___ no

4.3 PRIMARY ACTIVITY BOX

Fabulous phonicolours

ACTIVITY TYPE
individual pronunciation
activity

LANGUAGE FOCUS
pronunciation of simple
vocabulary

LEVEL
2

AGE RANGE
9–11

SKILLS
reading and distinguishing
sounds /eɪ/, /e/, /uː/,
/əʊ/, /ɪ/, /aɪ/, /ɒ/, /iː/,
/ɜː/, /æ/, /aʊ/

TIME
20–40 minutes

MATERIALS
a copy of the *Fabulous
phonicolours* worksheet per
pupil, crayons

Before class
Make a copy of the *Fabulous phonicolours* worksheet for each pupil.

In class
The idea of this exercise is to get learners to associate the vowel sounds in the names of the colours with the vowel sounds in certain words, identify these sounds and colour the words accordingly.

1 Check that your pupils know the names of the colours, in both their written and spoken forms.

2 Say *grey – day*, stressing the target sound /eɪ/. Say *Listen and repeat*. Repeat the words and listen to your pupils' response. Correct their pronunciation if necessary.

3 Say *Colour the box grey* and indicate where they should colour. Repeat the process for the other colours and sounds: red /e/, blue /uː/, pink /ɪ/, brown /aʊ/, purple /ɜː/, green /iː/, orange /ɒ/, white /aɪ/, black /æ/, yellow /əʊ/.

4 Refer your class to the first word in the grid of their exercise: *mouth*. Say the word, stressing the target sound /aʊ/, and name two colours for them to choose from. For example, say *Mouth. Green or brown?* and wait for your pupils to respond.

5 If the answer is right, say *Good. Mouth – brown*, stressing the target sound /aʊ/. Say *Colour the box brown*.

6 If the answer is wrong, say *Mouth – green?* Stress the two different sounds, /aʊ/ and /iː/, to contrast them so that your pupils can hear the difference.

7 Ask the class to continue colouring the boxes individually. Encourage them to say the words to themselves as they do this.

8 Circulate to monitor and help.

9 Correct the exercise orally.

Key
The key is given on p. 126.

Extension
Fast finishers can group the words in the exercise under the following headings: *Parts of the body, Clothes, Verbs, Other*.

Non-readers
If your pupils are weaker at reading, you can dictate the words and pupils can colour in the boxes.

Fabulous phonicolours

Say the words and colour the sounds.

grey day ☐   orange sock ☐   red bed ☐

green tree ☐   blue shoe ☐   purple worm ☐

yellow yo-yo ☐   black sack ☐   pink pig ☐

brown mouse ☐   white kite ☐

mouth		head		down			
queen		go		close			
fish		stop		desk			
toe		skirt		man			
egg		eight		time			
word		big		knee			
see		bike		clock			
two		cat		ten			
apple		coat		six			
moon		zoo		hand			
play		dress		nine			
eye		cake		girl			
hop		house		room			
nose		shirt		me			

4.4 PRIMARY ACTIVITY BOX

Space race

ACTIVITY TYPE
pairwork pronunciation
activity

LANGUAGE FOCUS
pronunciation and spelling
variants of words containing
the sound /eɪ/

LEVEL
3

AGE RANGE
10–11

SKILLS
reading, speaking

TIME
20–30 minutes

MATERIALS
a copy of the *Space race*
worksheet per pair, different
coloured pens or pencils

Before class
Make a copy of the *Space race* worksheet for each pair of pupils.

In class
1 Write *Space race* on the board. Read it aloud, stressing the pronunciation of the vowel sounds /eɪ/. Ask the class to give examples of other words that contain this sound.

2 Write the suggested words on the board. Ask the class collectively if they agree with each suggestion, saying *Is that right?*

3 If the suggestion is incorrect repeat the word, stressing the vowel sound, and repeat the title of the game, contrasting the sounds to show how they differ. Clean the word off the blackboard.

4 Continue to ask for suggestions until you feel that pupils have got a clear idea of the target sound. Clean the board.

5 Give pupils a copy of the photocopy per pair, and explain that they are going to play the game in pairs. With different coloured pens or pencils they take it in turns to identify the words that contain the target sound. Tell them that you will correct it later and that each correct answer gets two points and each incorrect answer gets minus one point (so as to discourage wild guesses).

6 Set a time limit of ten minutes.

7 When they have finished, or the time is up, correct the exercise collectively. Ask pupils to dictate the correct answers to you. Write the answers on the board in two columns, one for correct answers, and one for incorrect ones.

8 Pupils then add up their points to see who is the winner.

Key
(in alphabetical order)
break cake calculator date day eight face game grey make name page paper plate play rain say skate stay table take they train

Extension
Divide the class into groups of four to six and ask them to make lists of words that rhyme. Give groups points for the number of rhyming words they can find, i.e. skate, date – 2 points; skate, date, eight – 3 points; skate, date, eight, plate – 4 points

wear
paper
rabbit
page
salad

say
date
face
father
cup
table

cheese
cupboard
they
eight
bicycle

calculator
please
kite

ten
skate
make

desk
day
rain

cake
fat
milk

bed
ball
nose
cat

want
bread

tea
hear

ear
meat

boot
take
bag

night
name
meal
stair

me
bat
boat

plate
walk
bike
get

cinema
game
stay

chair
eat
grey

two
goat

play
train
apple
right
break
read
like

5.1 PRIMARY ACTIVITY BOX

In your classroom who ...?

ACTIVITY TYPE
whole class information gap activity

LANGUAGE FOCUS
Are you (happy)? Yes, I am./No, I'm not.
Can you (play football)? Yes, I can./No, I can't.
Have you got (a brother)? Yes, I have./No, I haven't.

LEVEL
2

AGE RANGE
8–11

SKILLS
speaking, listening for information, reading, writing

TIME
30 minutes

MATERIALS
a copy of the *In your classroom who ...?* worksheet per pupil

Before class

Before the class, complete the spaces on the photocopy with an age and place appropriate to your class, e.g.
Who is nine years old?
Who is from Brazil?
and make a copy of the *In your classroom who ...?* worksheet for each pupil.

In class

1 Write the following sentences on the board:
She is ten.
He can play tennis.
She has got a bike.

Ask your pupils to form questions (*Are you ten? Can you play tennis? Have you got a bike?*) and write these on the board.

2 Ask individual pupils these questions to elicit short answers (*Yes, I am. No, I can't.* etc.).

3 Give out the worksheets. Ask pupils to write the questions in the spaces provided. Tell them the last space in each section is for them to invent their own question.

4 Check with the whole class that they have written the correct questions:
Are you happy? Can you play football? Have you got a brother or sister? etc.

5 Using the first question as an example, demonstrate the activity. Ask a pupil *Are you happy?* If she answers *Yes, I am*, then write her name on your sheet. If not, write nothing and go on to another pupil. Tell your pupils that you want three names for each question.

6 Ask them to stand up and move around, asking each other the questions and writing down the names. Set a time limit.

7 Circulate to clarify, monitor and correct.

Extension

1 Using the answers your pupils have collected, you can create a chart to represent your class. This can either be done as a whole class activity or in smaller groups (six pupils per group).

2 If it is done in small groups then pupils draw a chart with the questions down the side and numbers along the bottom. Pupils then collect their answers together, and colour in squares according to the number of pupils who *are happy, can play football,* etc.

3 Help pupils with their charts, and display the completed charts on the walls.

Note

This kind of activity is especially suitable for adaptation. You can write similar surveys according to your class's level. More proficient groups can write their own questions.

For more practice on personal information see **1.2 All about me**
For more practice on these structures see **6.4 Sentence Bingo**

Who is happy?

Question: _____ you _____ ?

Who is _____ years old?

Question: _____

Who is from _____ ?

Question: _____

Question: _____

Who can play football?

Question: _____ you _____ ?

Who can ride a bike?

Question: _____

Who can speak English?

Question: _____

Question: _____

Who has got a brother?

Question: _____ you _____ ?

Who has got a red T-shirt?

Question: _____

Who has got a pet?

Question: _____

Question: _____

5.2

Identikit

PRIMARY ACTIVITY BOX

ACTIVITY TYPE
pairwork information gap

LANGUAGE FOCUS
have got/has got: question
forms and short answers
face parts: *hair, eyes, mouth,
nose*
adjectives: *short, long, blue,
brown, green, blond, black,
big, small*

LEVEL
2

AGE RANGE
8–11

SKILLS
speaking, listening for
information, reading, writing
(optional)

TIME
20–30 minutes depending on
pupils' ability

MATERIALS
a copy of the *Identikit*
worksheet per pair of pupils

Before class
Make a copy of the *Identikit* worksheet for every pair of pupils. Cut each copy into two parts:
A and B.

In class
1   Revise or pre-teach the adjectives for physical description used in the activity.

2   Copy the chart from the activity onto the board, substituting three of your pupils' names in
the left-hand column. Ask individual pupils questions to check that they understand the
procedure:
Has Paula got blue eyes?   No, she hasn't.
Has Paula got brown eyes?   Yes, she has.

3   Write *brown* in the appropriate box.

4   Arrange the class in pairs: A and B. Give pupils their section of the worksheet, A or B and
ask them to face their partners. Explain that the information on their photocopy is 'secret'
and pupils can only look at their own piece of paper. Let them read their sheet.

5   Pupils ask and answer questions to complete the sheet.

6   Circulate to monitor and correct.

Optional written work
1   Using the information in the chart, pupils write sentences about each character.

2   Write the example on the board:
Sarah has got long brown hair, green eyes, a small mouth and a long nose.

3   Pupils use this model to make sentences, reading them aloud to the teacher and class.

4   Once they have done the exercise orally they can proceed to write the sentences.

Extension 1
Pupils can draw pictures of each character using the completed descriptions in the table.

Extension 2
More advanced pupils can write a description of themselves. Remind them to use the correct
form – *I have got* – and tell them not to write their names on their paper. Collect the
descriptions, mix them up, and read them out for the class to guess who is being described.
Alternatively you could ask some pupils to each pick a description and read it out.

For more practice on *have/has got* see **5.6 Colour co-ordinates 6.4 Sentence Bingo
9.3 Dotty's puppies**

Identikit

A

Ask questions with *has got*.

Example: Has Sarah got a small nose?   No, she hasn't.
Has Mrs Jones got long hair?   Yes, she has.

	hair		eyes	mouth	nose
Simon	short		brown		big
Sarah		brown		small	long
Stephen	short				small
Susan	short		green	big	
Mrs Jones	long				
Mr Smith		black	blue	small	long

B

Ask questions with *has got*.

Example: Has Sarah got a small nose?   No, she hasn't.
Has Mrs Jones got long hair?   Yes, she has.

	hair		eyes	mouth	nose
Simon		blond		big	
Sarah	long		green		long
Stephen		brown	blue	small	
Susan		blond			small
Mrs Jones	long	black	brown	big	big
Mr Smith	short				

5.3

They can do it

PRIMARY ACTIVITY BOX

ACTIVITY TYPE
pairwork information gap

LANGUAGE FOCUS
can/can't: question forms and short answers

LEVEL
2

AGE RANGE
8–11

SKILLS
speaking, listening for information, reading, writing (optional)

TIME
20–30 minutes

MATERIALS
a copy of the *They can do it* worksheet per pair of pupils

Before class
Make a copy of the *They can do it* worksheet for every two pupils. Cut each copy in two parts: A and B.

In class
1 Revise or pre-teach *can* and the verbs used in the activity.

2 Copy the chart from the activity onto the board, substituting three of your pupils' names in the left-hand column. Ask individual pupils questions to check that they understand the procedure:
Petra, can you sing?   Yes, I can.
Juan, can you swim?   No, I can't.

3 Complete the chart with the answers they give you. Use ✓ for yes, and ✗ for no. Point to the *I* under the first three names and explain by demonstration that they must complete their own information. Say *I can sing. I can't swim.* and put a tick and a cross in the appropriate boxes. Draw their attention to the row with *you*, and explain that they ask their partners the questions using *Can you sing? Can you swim?* etc.

4 Arrange the class in pairs: A and B. Give pupils their section of the worksheet, A or B, and ask them to face their partners. Explain that the information on their photocopy is 'secret' and pupils can only look at their own piece of paper. Let them read their sheet.

5 Pupils first complete the information for themselves (in the *I* row) then ask and answer questions to complete the sheet.

6 Circulate to monitor and correct.

Optional written work
1 Using the information in the chart pupils write sentences about each character. This is particularly effective as a graded completion exercise used to practise conjunctions *and*, *but* and *or*. Write the example on the board: *Simon can sing, swim **and** climb trees, **but** he can't play the piano **or** ride a bike.*

2 Ask pupils to use this model to make up similar sentences and say them aloud to the teacher and class. They also make sentences about 'My friend'. Insist on the use of *and*, *but* and *or*.

3 Once they have done the exercise orally they can proceed to write the sentences.

For more practice on *can* see **6.4 Sentence Bingo 9.2 Where are they sitting?**

They can do it

A

Ask questions with *can*.   *Example:* Can Simon climb trees?   Yes, he can.
Can Julie play the piano? No, she can't.

	sing	swim	play the piano	climb trees	ride a bike
Simon		✗	✓	✓	
Julie	✗		✗	✓	
Mrs Lee	✓	✗			✓
I					
You					

B

Ask questions with *can*.   *Example:* Can Simon climb trees?   Yes, he can.
Can Julie play the piano? No, she can't.

	sing	swim	play the piano	climb trees	ride a bike
Simon	✗			✓	✓
Julie		✓	✗		✗
Mrs Lee			✓	✗	
I					
You					

5.4 PRIMARY ACTIVITY BOX

Room for improvement

ACTIVITY TYPE
pairwork: 'spot the difference' information gap

LANGUAGE FOCUS
there is/are
prepositions of place
clothes, toys, classroom objects, furniture

LEVEL
3

AGE RANGE
9–11

SKILLS
listening, speaking, writing (optional)

TIME
50 minutes

MATERIALS
a copy of the *Room for improvement* worksheet per pair of pupils

Before class

Make a copy of the *Room for improvement* worksheet for every two pupils. Cut each copy in two parts: A and B.

In class

1 Check comprehension of the basic structures required for the exercise by asking questions about the classroom, e.g.
Is there a window?   Yes, there is.
Is there a pencil next to my book?   No, there isn't. etc.

2 Revise or pre-teach the prepositions and vocabulary used in the activity.

3 Explain how the activity works by example. Select a pupil and sit facing him or her. Give the pupil the 'B' picture and you keep the 'A' picture. Ask *Are there some trousers on the chair?* to elicit the response *No, there are some trousers under the bed.* Tell the class that there are another nine differences.

4 Arrange the class in pairs: A and B. Give pupils their section of the worksheet, A or B, and ask them to face their partners. Explain that the information on their photocopy is 'secret' and pupils can only look at their own piece of paper. Let them look at their sheet. Pupils then ask each other questions to find the differences and mark these on their sheets.

5 Set a suitable time limit for the task. When pupils have finished, ask them to compare their sheets to check the answers.

Key

	Picture A	*Picture B*		*Picture A*	*Picture B*
shirt	in the cupboard	under the table	train	on the shelf	on the floor
shoes	in the cupboard	on the bed	book	on the table	on the bed
ball	on the shelf	on the floor	plane	on the table	under the chair
car	on the shelf	under the bed	apple	on the table	on the chair
			glass	on the table	on the floor

Optional written work

1 In pairs, pupils write about their pictures, describing the differences. Tell them to divide their page into two columns and label them *Picture A* and *Picture B*, and write a sentence in each column to describe the difference, e.g.

Picture A
The trousers are on the chair.
OR
There are some trousers on the chair.

Picture B
The trousers are under the bed.

There are some trousers under the bed.

2 When they have finished, they dictate the sentences for you to write on the board. They correct their sentences accordingly.

Extension

Pupils draw a picture of their own room and write five sentences to describe it.

For more practice on prepositions see **3.4 Colourful cans**
For more practice on *there is/are* see **9.5 Shaping up**

Room for improvement

A Can you find ten differences?

B Can you find ten differences?

5.5

PRIMARY ACTIVITY BOX

You read, I write

ACTIVITY TYPE
pairwork dictation

LANGUAGE FOCUS
verbs *to be, have got*
vocabulary for physical
description
toys
brother, sister
Can you repeat that please?
Can you spell that please?

LEVEL
2

AGE RANGE
8–10

SKILLS
reading, listening, speaking

TIME
20–30 minutes

MATERIALS
a copy of the *You read, I write*
worksheet per two pupils

Before class

Make a copy of the *You read, I write* worksheet for every two pupils. Cut each copy in two parts: A and B.

In class

1 Revise or pre-teach the questions *Can you repeat that please?* and *Can you spell that please?* and write them on the board.

2 Explain how the activity works by example. Select a pupil and sit facing him or her. Give the pupil the 'B' dictation and you keep the 'A' dictation.

3 Ask the pupil to read his or her text while you write the missing words. Once you have filled in the spaces in your text, read your text so that your partner can write his or her missing words. Demonstrate or explain that you need to say *Blank* or *Mmmm* to indicate where there is a gap. Take turns to read and write. After one or two lines check that the class understand the task.

4 Arrange the class in pairs: A and B. Give pupils their section of the worksheet, A or B, and ask them to face their partners. Explain that the information on their photocopy is 'secret' and pupils can only look at their own piece of paper. Let them read their sheet.

5 Pupils read and write to complete their sheets.

6 Circulate to monitor and correct.

7 When pupils have finished, either they can check their answers in pairs, or ask them to dictate the text for you to write on the board.

Key

This is the complete text:

My friend's name is Suzy. She is seven years old. She's got a brother and a sister. Her brother's name is Simon and her sister's name is Stella.

Suzy's got blue eyes and brown hair. Her hair is very short. She isn't tall and she isn't fat. She's a happy girl.

She's got a lot of toys. She's got three cars, a red ball and a doll. Her favourite toy is her doll.

8 Finally ask some comprehension questions to make sure that everyone understands the text, e.g.
How old is Suzy?
What colour is her hair?
How many cars has she got?

Option

You can make posters of typical classroom language to display on the walls, e.g.
Can you repeat that please?
Can you spell that please?
I don't understand.

For more practice on physical descriptions and possessives see **9.3 Dotty's puppies**

A

My friend's name .... Suzy. She is .... years old . ...

.... a brother and .... Her brother's ....

Simon and .... sister's name is Stella.

Suzy's got .... and brown hair. ....

very short. .... tall and she isn't .... She's a .... girl.

.... a lot of toys. She's got ...., a red ....

.... doll. Her favourite .... is her ....

use

Can you repeat that please?
Can you spell that please?

B

My .... is Suzy . ... seven years ....

She's got .... and a sister. .... brother's name is Simon

.... her sister's .... Stella.

.... blue eyes and .... Her hair is very

.... She isn't .... and .... fat. She's a happy

....

She's got a lot of .... three cars, a .... ball and

a .... favourite toy .... her doll.

use

Can you repeat that please?
Can you spell that please?

5.6

PRIMARY ACTIVITY BOX

Colour co-ordinates

ACTIVITY TYPE
pairwork information gap

LANGUAGE FOCUS
have got: question forms and
short answers
word order
colours
clothes

LEVEL
2

AGE RANGE
7–11

SKILLS
speaking, listening for
information, reading, writing

TIME
30 minutes

MATERIALS
a copy of the *Colour
co-ordinates* worksheet per
pair of pupils

Before class
Make a copy of the *Colour co-ordinates* worksheet for every two pupils. Cut each copy in two parts: A and B.

In class
1 Revise or pre-teach colours and the clothes vocabulary used in the activity.

2 Copy the chart from the activity onto the board to show how it works. Say *I've got a blue T-shirt*, pointing to the intersection between 'blue' and 'T-shirt' marked with a ✓. Point to a similarly marked intersection and say *I've got …* pausing to allow pupils to suggest the answer. Ensure that you practise with both singular and plural nouns, checking that they use or omit the indefinite article where appropriate. Clean the board.

3 Explain how the activity works by example. Select a pupil and sit facing him or her. Give the pupil the 'B' chart and you keep the 'A' chart. Say *Peter, have you got a green sweater?* to elicit the response *No, I haven't.* Your pupil then asks you another question. Emphasise the question form *Have you got …?* and the short answers *Yes, I have./No, I haven't.* Write these as prompts on the board if necessary.

4 Arrange the class in pairs: A and B. Give pupils their section of the worksheet, A or B, and ask them to face their partners. Explain that the information on their photocopy is 'secret' and pupils can only look at their own piece of paper.

5 Give pupils a maximum number of questions each (ten for example) and allow them to proceed with the game. They take it in turns to ask and answer questions to get the information.

6 Circulate to monitor and correct. The pupil in each pair who finds the most articles is the winner.

Optional written work
Using the information about their partners, pupils write sentences beginning 'He/She's got …' in their notebooks. Correct these sentences collectively on the board.

Option
If you prefer, you can delete the ticks on the master copy with correcting fluid to allow pupils to tick their own co-ordinates.

Non-readers
If your pupils are non-readers, you may wish to colour in the boxes in the left-hand column with the appropriate colours to enable your pupils to do the activity without needing to read the text.

For more practice on clothes vocabulary see **2.4 Join the dots 6.5 Cowboy dot-to-dot 7.1 Jack and Jill**

Colour co-ordinates

PRIMARY ACTIVITY BOX 5.6

A

	T-shirt	trousers	shoes	shorts	sweater
green			✔		
yellow		✔			
red				✔	
blue	✔				
brown					✔

✂ -

B

	T-shirt	trousers	shoes	shorts	sweater
green	✔				
yellow				✔	
red			✔		
blue					✔
brown		✔			

From *Primary Activity Box* by C. Nixon and M. Tomlinson © Cambridge University Press 2001 **PHOTOCOPIABLE**   75

6.1

PRIMARY ACTIVITY BOX

Whose is it?

ACTIVITY TYPE
individual matching and
colouring exercise

LANGUAGE FOCUS
possessive 's
Whose …?
verb *to be*
classroom objects

LEVEL
1

AGE RANGE
5–8

SKILLS
speaking, writing (optional)

TIME
20–30 minutes

MATERIALS
a copy of the *Whose is it?*
worksheet per pupil, crayons

Before class

Make a copy of the *Whose is it?* worksheet for each pupil.

In class

1 Pre-teach or revise *pen, pencil, rubber, ruler, bag, book, calculator, cassette, shoe, (pencil) sharpener*.

2 Select four pupils from your class with names whose initial letters correspond to the initial letter of two objects, e.g.

| Carol | cat | Mary | map | Ben | ball | Henry | horse |
| | car | | mouse | | bike | | house |

3 Write the words on the blackboard in circles and the four names down the side.

4 Say *Whose cat is it?* and point to the names in turn emphasising the letter. Elicit *It's Carol's cat* and write both question and answer on the board.

5 Repeat the procedure with other objects, checking for correct use and pronunciation of the possessive 's.

6 When pupils have got the idea, give out a copy of the worksheet to each pupil. Decide the characters' names collectively by general consensus – encourage pupils to think of English names. Write the names on the board.

7 In pairs pupils then do the exercise orally, asking and answering as above.

8 Circulate to monitor and correct.

9 Pupils then colour the letters on the T-shirts the same colour as the object that belongs to that character. Alternatively, with younger pupils, you can ask them to draw a line to connect the character to the objects.

Optional written work

Older pupils can write out the questions and answers for the ten objects.

Extension

Pupils choose four names and eight objects and make up their own exercise in the same way as above. They can use this with a partner or the teacher can keep them for use at a later date.

Note

If you feel the letter 'S' on the girl's T-shirt will cause confusion in relation to 'shoe' and 'sharpener' because of the different sounds, you may like to call her Sharon, Sheila, Shirley or Sheena, etc.

For more practice on classroom vocabulary see **1.3 My classroom friend**
For more practice on possessives see **7.1 Jack and Jill 8.5 Dress me up**

Gramminoes

ACTIVITY TYPE
matching dominoes game for pairs or small groups

LANGUAGE FOCUS
personal pronouns
to be
adjectives to describe people and things

LEVEL
2

AGE RANGE
8–11

SKILLS
reading, speaking, writing (optional)

TIME
20 minutes

MATERIALS
a copy of the *Gramminoes* worksheet per pair or small group

Before class

Make a copy of the *Gramminoes* worksheet per pair or small group. Cut the photocopy into 21 'grammino' cards.

In class

1 Arrange the class in pairs or small groups working around a table.

2 Explain the rules. This can be done by example. Shuffle the cards and divide them between the pupils. Turn the last card over and place it in the middle of the table.

3 The player to the left of the dealer starts. He or she puts a card next to the card on the table (either before or after). It must fit grammatically and logically. Encourage pupils to say the sentence as they put their gramminoes down.

4 The player on the left continues, and repeats the process. If any one player cannot put a grammino down then it is the next player's turn.

5 The first person to play all his or her gramminoes is the winner. If no more gramminoes can be put down at any point in the game, the winner is the player with the least gramminoes in his or her hand.

6 Encourage pupils to use English for communicating while they play. Teach them phrases such as *Whose turn is it? It's my turn. Can you go? That's not right. Is that right? I'm the winner.*

Optional written work

1 Pupils write the sentences that are made during the game.

2 Circulate to monitor and correct.

3 Ask pupils to read out the sentences they have made and write them on the board. Correct the sentences collectively.

Extension

More advanced pupils can make similar sentences and transfer them to the *Dominoes* template on p. 122 to make up their own game.

For another dominoes game see **1.6 Instructions dominoes**. You can also use the *Dominoes* template on p. 122 to create your own dominoes game.

boy	It's a short	pencil	He's a young	boy	It's a big
boys	They're old	men	They're thin	women	I'm a tall
girl	She's an old	woman	He's a fat	man	It's a small
chair	We're big	girls	They're thin	boys	I'm a young
child	She's a happy	girl	They're long	pencils	We're clever
children	I'm a clever	child	He's a fat	baby	They're sad
babies	We're young	girls	I'm a small	table	We're happy

Which sweet?

ACTIVITY TYPE
individual question and
answer matching and
colouring activity

LANGUAGE FOCUS
question forms with verb *to be*:
How many …?
How old …?
What …?
Where …?

LEVEL
3

AGE RANGE
7–10

SKILLS
reading

TIME
20 minutes

MATERIALS
a copy of the *Which sweet?*
worksheet per pupil, crayons

Before class
Make a copy of the *Which sweet?* worksheet for each pupil.

In class

1   Give out a copy of the worksheet to each pupil. Ask your pupils to read the information in silence.

2   Draw four or five 'sweets' on the blackboard or an OHT. Write *What's your name?* in the centre of one, and GREY in the outer circle. Write the correct answer in the centre of one of the other sweets and incorrect answers in the centre of the others.

3   When the class has finished reading, draw their attention to the 'sweets' on the board and read *What's your name?* aloud. Point to an incorrect answer and say, *They're under the bed. – Is that right?* Give pupils the opportunity to respond, then repeat the process, choosing another incorrect answer and asking the class if it is the right solution.

4   Continue this procedure until they have got the idea, then point to the correct answer and say *My name's Robert.* When your class answer affirmatively, say *Good* and pick up a grey crayon or pencil and mime colouring the outer ring.

5   Ask pupils to complete the worksheet individually.

6   Circulate to monitor and help.

7   The activity can be corrected individually by the teacher or collectively by asking pupils to read out the correct question and answer combinations.

Key

How old are you? I'm nine. (pink)
What's this? It's a ruler. (blue)
Where are my shoes? They're under the bed. (red)
What are those? They're pens. (yellow)
How old are they? They're ten. (green)
How are you? I'm fine, thanks. (orange)
Where's my pencil? It's on the table. (brown)
What colour are Simon's shoes? They're brown. (purple)
What colour's your T-shirt? It's blue. (black)
How many chairs are there? There are six. (white)
What's your name? My name's Robert. (grey)

Option
On separate pieces of card, write out these questions and answers and more if necessary so that you have enough cards for each pupil in your class. Give pupils one card each and ask them to move around the classroom to find their other half.

For more question and answer practice see **5.1 In your classroom who …?** There is also a **Which sweet?** template on p. 123 so that you can repeat the activity, practising questions of your own choice.

Colour the pairs.

Sentence Bingo

ACTIVITY TYPE
whole class Bingo game

LANGUAGE FOCUS
verbs *to be, can, have got*
basic adjectives of
appearance
toys
age

LEVEL
2

AGE RANGE
7–9

SKILLS
listening, reading

TIME
30–40 minutes

MATERIALS
two copies of the Teacher's
baseboard, one copy of
pupils' Bingo cards per ten
pupils, nine paper squares
per pupil

Before class

The photocopy consists of ten pupils' Bingo cards and one Teacher's baseboard. Each pupils' card has nine boxes. Each horizontal line is a simple sentence. The Teacher's baseboard consists of 36 boxes.

Make two photocopies of the Teacher's baseboard, each on different coloured paper or card. Leave one sheet intact as the baseboard, and cut the other one up into individual pieces and keep these safely in a small bag.

Make a photocopy (enlarged if possible) of the pupils' Bingo cards for each ten pupils and cut it into individual cards of three sentences. Each pupil will need one card and either nine paper squares to cover their boxes or a pencil to cross them off.

In class

1   Explain any vocabulary if necessary. Give out the Bingo cards and ask your pupils to study them for a few minutes to familiarise themselves with the language content.

2   Explain that you are going to call out some words and if they have those words on their card, they should cross them off in pencil, or cover them with a square of paper. When they have crossed off a complete horizontal 'line' (a sentence) they must call out 'line' and read the sentence back to you. If it is correct they will win five points. Demonstrate on the board if necessary.

3   Explain that after the first 'line' has been called, they should continue playing for 'Bingo'. The first pupil to cover or tick all the squares on his/her card wins fifteen points.

4   Start the game by saying *Eyes down* and gesture by bending your head to look at the board. Your pupils now have the cue which signals the start of the game. They should be looking at their cards and paying attention.

5   Mix up your bag of words and phrases. Take the first one out and read it aloud twice. Place it on the corresponding part of your baseboard and continue in this way. Be careful that pupils do not see the teacher's word in its written form, as this is primarily a listening exercise.

6   The winner must read the sentences aloud for you to check on your baseboard. Check both pronunciation and intonation (pupils tend to read the individual components back to you as though they were calling 'Bingo', rather than reading a sentence).

Option

More advanced pupils can make their own Bingo game as follows.

1   Divide your class into pairs and give them a photocopy of the Teacher's baseboard per pair. Set them a time limit to make their own Bingo cards of three sentences with three components in each, without repeating any one component.

2   Circulate to help and check.

3   When they have completed the task proceed to play Bingo as above.

For more practice on these structures see **5.1 In your classroom who ...? 5.5 You read, I write**

There is a **Bingo** template on p. 124 so that you can repeat the activity, practising sentences of your own choice.

Sentence Bingo

We	can	sing	We	can	dance
He	has got	a balloon	You	aren't	sad
I	am	short	He	isn't	nine

They	can't	dance	I	am not	a boy
I	am	a girl	She	hasn't got	a doll
She	has got	long hair	They	are	children

I	am not	ten	I	am	happy
You	have got	long hair	He	is	a boy
She	isn't	sad	We	have got	short hair

They	can't	sing	He	is	happy
She	hasn't got	blue eyes	We	haven't got	a car
You	are	tall	They	aren't	tall

You	aren't	nine	She	has got	a bike
He	hasn't got	short hair	We	are	children
They	haven't got	blue eyes	I	am not	short

TEACHER'S BASEBOARD						
	I	am	am not	dance	a bike	a girl
	You	can	can't	short	a car	short hair
	He	are	aren't	happy	a balloon	long hair
	She	is	isn't	ten	sing	blue eyes
	We	has got	hasn't got	a boy	tall	a doll
	They	have got	haven't got	children	sad	nine

Cowboy dot-to-dot

ACTIVITY TYPE
individual 'join the dots'
dictation

LANGUAGE FOCUS
the present continuous
Yes, he is./No, he isn't.
possessive *'s*
clothes
colours

LEVEL
2

AGE RANGE
8–10

SKILLS
reading, listening, controlled
writing, speaking

TIME
30–45 minutes

MATERIALS
a copy of the *Cowboy dot-to-dot* worksheet per pupil,
crayons

Before class
Make a copy of the *Cowboy dot-to-dot* worksheet for each pupil.

In class
1 Pre-teach *scarf, mask* and *waistcoat* and any other vocabulary that your pupils do not know.

2 Give each pupil a copy of the worksheet and explain that they should put their pencils on the word *This* to begin with (next to the pencil symbol on their worksheet) and then draw lines joining the words they hear. Do an example on the blackboard to demonstrate.

3 Play the cassette or read the tapescript. Pupils listen first to the whole sentence. Then they listen to the paused version and draw the lines from dot to dot. Finally they listen to the whole sentence again to check.

Tapescript – Listening 1

This boy is sitting in front of the television. He is watching a very good film. It is about a cowboy.

4 Point to the sentence at the bottom of the page and draw pupils' attention to punctuation. Remind them that a capital letter comes after a full stop. Ask them to complete the sentence. It is the same as the sentence dictated.

5 Correct the activity collectively. Write the correct sentences on the blackboard for pupils to correct their own work.

6 Ask pupils the following questions about the picture.

1 What's the boy doing?	7 Is the boy wearing a hat?
2 Is the boy wearing a T-shirt?	8 What's the boy wearing?
3 Is the man wearing a mask?	9 Is the man wearing a hat?
4 Is the man wearing a waistcoat?	10 Is the man wearing glasses?
5 Is the man wearing a scarf?	11 Is the man sleeping?
6 Is the man wearing a shirt?	12 What's the man wearing?

7 Now do the following colour dictation. Play the cassette or read the tapescript and pupils colour as instructed. Pause the cassette after each sentence to give them time to colour.

Tapescript – Listening 2

Colour the boy's socks yellow. Colour the boy's shoes brown.
Colour the boy's shorts grey. Colour the boy's T-shirt green.
Colour the boy's hair orange. Colour the cowboy's hat black.
Colour the cowboy's shirt red. Colour the cowboy's waistcoat blue.
Colour the cowboy's scarf purple. Colour the television pink.

Non-readers
If your pupils are non-readers or weaker at reading, you may prefer to number the words from 1 to 21 on a master copy before making your pupils' worksheets.

For more practice on possessives and clothes see **7.1 Jack and Jill 8.5 Dress me up**

Cowboy dot-to-dot

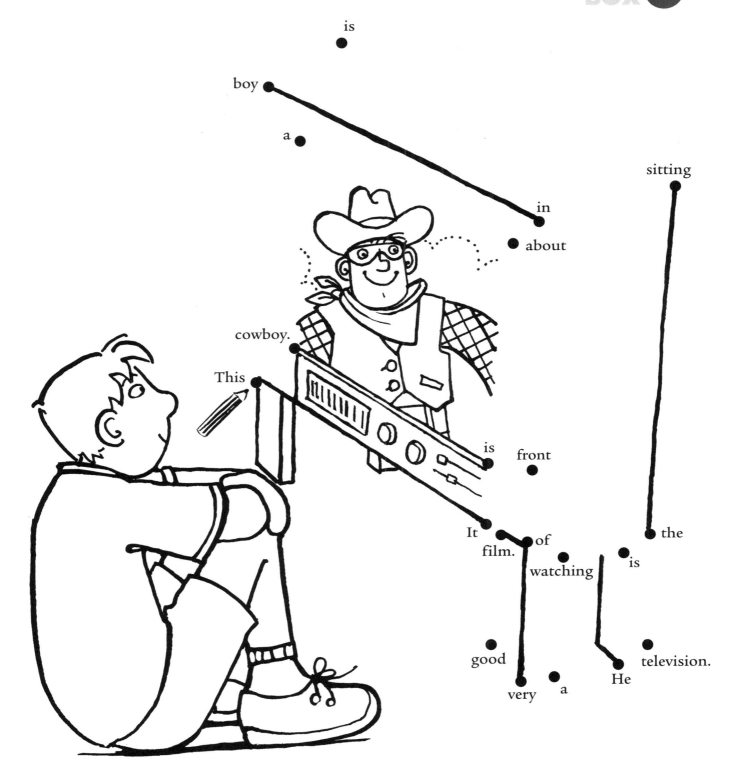

is

boy

a

sitting

in

about

cowboy.

This

is   front

It   of
film.   watching   is

good   the

very   a   He   television.

_____ _____ _____ sitting _____ _____ of

_____ television . _____ _____ _____ a very

_____ _____ . It _____ about _____ _____ .

7.1 PRIMARY ACTIVITY BOX

Jack and Jill

ACTIVITY TYPE
song, individual colour
dictation

LANGUAGE FOCUS
clothes vocabulary
possessive 's
colours

LEVEL
1

AGE RANGE
5–8

SKILLS
listening, speaking

TIME
50–60 minutes

MATERIALS
one (enlarged) copy of the
Jack and Jill flashcard, a copy
of the *Jack and Jill* worksheet
per pupil, cassette (optional),
crayons

Before class

Make a copy of the *Jack and Jill* photocopy per pupil. If you have a large class you might also want to make a copy of the flashcard for each pupil so that everyone will be able to see it clearly.

In class

1 Show the class the flashcard and say *Look at these children. He's Jack and she's Jill.* Talk about the picture, practising key vocabulary (*Jack, Jill, hill, pail, crown*). Ask questions about the picture, e.g.
What's her name? What's his name? What have they got in their hands? What are they doing? What's this? What colour's this/the …? etc.

2 Say *Listen.* Play the song on cassette or sing it from the tapescript.

Tapescript – Listening 1

Jack and Jill went up the hill
To fetch a pail of water.
Jack fell down and broke his crown
And Jill came tumbling after.

3 Say *Listen and repeat.* Play the song again for pupils to repeat line by line. Check for pronunciation difficulties, especially the pronunciation of J and H, and correct if necessary.

4 Put actions to the song with younger learners. They mime 'up' and 'hill' with their arms, a bucket (pail) being pulled out of a well, 'Jack fell down and broke his crown' – the boys drop down onto the floor and rub their head with a look of pain and the girls do the same for 'Jill came tumbling after'.

5 Give pupils a copy of the worksheet. Play the cassette or read the tapescript. Give them time to colour before going on to the next instruction.

Tapescript – Listening 2

Colour Jack's shirt blue. Colour Jill's dress yellow.
Colour Jack's socks blue and purple.
Colour Jack's trousers purple. Colour Jill's shoes pink.
Colour Jack's shoes black. Colour Jack's hair orange.
Colour Jill's hair brown. Colour the pail grey.
Colour the hill green. Colour the path brown.
Colour the well red.

For more practice on possessives and clothes see **6.5 Cowboy dot-to-dot**
8.5 Dress me up

From *Primary Activity Box* by C. Nixon and M. Tomlinson © Cambridge University Press 2001

Incy Wincy Spider

ACTIVITY TYPE
action song, individual story sequencing, colouring

LANGUAGE FOCUS
basic weather vocabulary and pronunciation

LEVEL
2

AGE RANGE
7–9

SKILLS
listening, speaking, reading

TIME
50–60 minutes

MATERIALS
one (enlarged) copy of the *Incy Wincy Spider* flashcard, a copy of the *Incy Wincy Spider* worksheet per pupil, cassette (optional), crayons

Before class

Make a copy of the *Incy Wincy Spider* worksheet for each pupil. Make an enlarged copy of the flashcard and colour it attractively. If you have a large class, you might also want to make a copy of the flashcard for each pupil so that everyone will be able to see it clearly.

In class

1 Show the class the flashcard and talk about the picture; pre-teach and practise key vocabulary: *spider, climb, spout, rain, sunshine, dry.* (The 'spout' in the song refers to what we would normally call a 'drainpipe'.) Ask questions e.g.
Who is he? What is he? What's he doing in the picture? Where is he going? Is it sunny? etc.

2 Play the cassette or sing from the tapescript. It also works well as a rhyme.

Tapescript

Incy Wincy Spider climbed up the spout.
Down came the rain and washed poor Incy out.
Out came the sunshine and dried up all the rain.
So Incy Wincy Spider climbed up the spout again.

3 Say *Listen and repeat* and practise the song line by line.

4 Demonstrate the following actions to the class, as in the photos on p. 128:

a *Incy Wincy Spider climbed up the spout* – put your left thumb against your right forefinger and then your right thumb against your left forefinger and keep repeating this, gradually raising your arms in a climbing movement

b *Down came the rain …* – start with your hands straight up above your head and gradually lower them, palms down, while wiggling your fingers to represent rain falling

c *… and washed poor Incy out* – dramatically sweep your hands downwards and outwards

d *Out came the sunshine …* – open your arms in a wide circle over your head

e *… and dried up all the rain* – same as 'down came the rain' but in the opposite direction

f *So Incy Wincy Spider climbed up the spout again* – repeat the original climbing movement

5 Ask the class to stand up and sing the song with the accompanying actions while you circulate to help, monitor and correct pronunciation.

6 Ask the class to sit down and give them the worksheet. Ask them to number the pictures in the correct order. Correct orally, explaining the sequence using weather vocabulary.

Key

The order is: c, d, b, a.

7 For the second exercise (large spider) pupils must colour the picture with colours that rhyme with the words (zoo = blue etc.). Demonstrate by example if necessary.

8 Circulate to monitor, prompt and help. Correct the exercise orally.

 From *Primary Activity Box* by C. Nixon and M. Tomlinson © Cambridge University Press 2001

Incy Wincy Spider

Write the numbers.

a ☐   b ☐   c ☐   d ☐

Now colour the picture.

7.3 ~~PRIMARY ACTIVITY BOX~~

Lucy Locket

ACTIVITY TYPE
action rhyme, individual sound differentiation activity

LANGUAGE FOCUS
basic vocabulary and its pronunciation: /ɒ/, /ɔː/, /ɜː/, /iː/

LEVEL
2

AGE RANGE
7–10

SKILLS
listening, speaking, reading, writing

TIME
50–60 minutes

MATERIALS
one (enlarged) copy of the *Lucy Locket* flashcard, a copy of the *Lucy Locket* worksheet per pupil, cassette (optional)

Before class

Make a copy of the *Lucy Locket* worksheet for each pupil. Make an enlarged copy of the flashcard and colour it attractively. If you have a large class, you might also want to make a copy of the flashcard for each pupil so that everyone will be able to see it clearly.

In class

1   Show the class the flashcard and say: *This is Lucy Locket*. Talk about the picture, pre-teach and practise key vocabulary: *lock, door, turn, key*. Ask questions about the picture, e.g. *What's her name? What's she got in her hand? What's she doing? Where's she going?* etc.

2   Say *Listen*. Play the cassette or read the tapescript.

Tapescript

When Lucy Locket goes to tea
She locks the door and turns the key.

3   Pupils listen and repeat line by line. Check for pronunciation difficulties.

4   Form pairs and ask one of your more outgoing pupils to come to the front to demonstrate the following actions with you (illustrated in the photos on p. 128):
    – Stand side by side, facing the same direction. Put your arms behind your back and take your pupil's right hand in yours and his/her left hand in yours.
    – Skip forwards a few steps in time to the rhyme and when you say *turns the key*, turn towards the outside, slightly pushing your pupil towards his/her outside as you do so without letting go of the hands.
    – You should now both be facing the opposite direction, ready to say the rhyme again.

5   Ask the class to stand up and skip a few steps as they repeat the rhyme, while you circulate to help, monitor and correct pronunciation.

6   Ask the class to sit down and look at the board. Write the words *lock, door, turn, key*. Say each word individually, stressing the target sounds for the class to repeat after you.

7   Say *Tree – lock, door, turn or key?* Wait for the class to discover the similarity between the sounds and to offer an answer. If the answer is correct, say *Good. Tree – key*, and write *tree* under *key* on the blackboard. If the answer is incorrect, say *Tree – lock?* (depending on the incorrect word they have chosen). Stress and contrast the target sounds so that your pupils can hear the difference.

8   Give out the worksheet. The exercise consists of writing the words in the correct columns, depending on their sounds. Circulate to monitor, prompt and help.

9   Correct the exercise collectively. Write the words in the correct columns on the board.

Key

The key is given on p. 127.

Non-readers

If your pupils are non-readers or weaker at reading, you may prefer to do the activity orally. Copy the pictures at the top of each column of the worksheet onto the board and stress their target sounds. Say each word and the class decides which sound group it belongs to.

lock	door	turn	key

purple   queen   morning   body   four

we   cheese   horse   bottle   dirty

stop   jeans   eat   bird   sport

daughter   teeth   shirt   north   box

clean   clock   water   thirty   circle   hot

fox   three   her   short   Thursday   sock

PRIMARY ACTIVITY BOX
My fish tank

ACTIVITY TYPE
song, individual 'make and do' activity

LANGUAGE FOCUS
numbers 1–10
left, right
colours

LEVEL
1

AGE RANGE
5–8

SKILLS
listening, speaking, reading

TIME
45 minutes

MATERIALS
one (enlarged) copy of the *My fish tank* flashcard, two copies of the *My fish tank* worksheet per pupil (see below) correcting fluid, scissors, glue, crayons, a small piece of sticking plaster for each pupil (optional), cassette (optional)

Before class

First make a master photocopy of the worksheet. Then use correcting fluid to erase the numbers inside the fish. Make a new photocopy and write numbers 1–10 in numerals inside the fish, making sure they do not correspond to the original numbers. You will need one copy with words and one copy with numerals for each pupil. Make an enlarged copy of the flashcard and colour it attractively. Alternatively, make a copy of the flashcard for each pupil.

In class

1 Show the class the flashcard. Talk about the pictures. Pre-teach and practise key vocabulary: *fish, finger, bite, left, right*, numbers 1–10. Ask questions about the four pictures, e.g.
What's the boy doing? What's this? What's he got in his hand? What's the fish doing? etc.

2 Say *Listen*. Play the cassette or sing from the tapescript. It also works as a rhyme.

Tapescript – Listening 1

One, two, three, four, five,	Why did you let it go?
Once I caught a fish alive.	Because it bit my finger so.
Six, seven, eight, nine, ten,	Which finger did it bite?
Then I let it go again.	This little finger on my right.

3 Practise the song line by line. Check for pronunciation difficulties and correct if necessary. Finally pupils stand up and sing the whole song.

4 Give pupils a copy of the second photocopy (numerals not words). Play the cassette or read the tapescript and ask them to colour the fish. Pause after each sentence to give them time.

Tapescript – Listening 2

Colour number nine grey. Colour number ten white. Colour number three orange. Colour number six green. Colour number one brown. Colour number eight red. Colour number seven yellow. Colour number five black. Colour number four purple. Colour number two pink.

5 Pupils cut out the fish. Give them a copy of the original photocopy (words). Pupils stick the fish onto the sheet matching the numerals to the words. They can then colour the background (blues/greens) to make it look like a fish tank.

Extension

1 Ask pupils to draw around both hands on a large piece of card and to write 'my left hand' and 'my right hand' across the palms.

2 Ask them to number the fingers, starting from their little left finger and finishing at their right little finger. They then write the numbers in words along each finger.

3 Give them a small piece of sticking plaster and ask them to listen to the song again and stick the plaster on the appropriate finger.

Non-readers

If you don't want to teach the words for the numbers, you could delete the words and do the activity using only numeral worksheets.

For more practice on numbers 1–10 see **2.6 Rainy days**

My fish tank flashcard

 From *Primary Activity Box* by C. Nixon and M. Tomlinson © Cambridge University Press 2001

My fish tank

PRIMARY ACTIVITY BOX
Diddle diddle dumpling

ACTIVITY TYPE
rhyme, individual sound differentiation activity

LANGUAGE FOCUS
sounds /ɒ/, /aʊ/, /uː/

LEVEL
3

AGE RANGE
8–11

SKILLS
speaking, listening, reading, writing

TIME
20–30 minutes

MATERIALS
one (enlarged) copy of the *Diddle diddle dumpling* flashcard, a copy of the *Diddle diddle dumpling* worksheet per pupil, orange, brown and blue crayons, cassette (optional)

Before class
Make a copy of the *Diddle diddle dumpling* worksheet for each pupil. Make an enlarged copy of the flashcard and colour it attractively. If you have a large class, you might also want to make a copy of the flashcard for each pupil so that everyone will be able to see it clearly.

In class
1 Show the class the flashcard and say: *Look, he's John. Who is he?* Talk about the picture to pre-teach and practise key vocabulary: *John, trousers, shoe.* Ask questions about the picture:
What's his name? Where is he? What is he doing? Who's looking at him? What's he wearing? What's this? What colour's this/the ...? etc.

2 Say *Listen.* Play the cassette or read the tapescript.

Tapescript
Diddle diddle dumpling my son John
Went to bed with his trousers on,
One shoe off and one shoe on,
Diddle diddle dumpling my son John.

3 Say *Listen and repeat* and practise the rhyme line by line. Check for pronunciation difficulties and correct if necessary. Finally pupils stand up and say the whole rhyme.

4 Pre-teach or revise the words from the worksheet.

5 Ask the class to look at the board. Say *Listen and repeat.* Say *John,* stressing the target sound /ɒ/ for the class to repeat after you.

6 Draw a bottle and a door with a circle next to each on the blackboard. Pointing to the words, say *John – bottle or door?* Wait for the class to discover the similarity between the sounds and to offer an answer. If the answer is correct, say *Good. John – bottle,* and colour in the circle next to the bottle.

7 If the answer is incorrect, say *John – door?* Stress and contrast the target sounds (/ɒ/, /ɔː/) so that your pupils can hear the difference.

8 Repeat this procedure with other words containing the target sound that are not on the worksheet (dog, clock; room, floor; flower, mouth; your, hour; you, glue; go, cup, etc.) until your pupils have a clear idea of the object of the exercise.

9 Give out the worksheets and ask pupils to do the exercises individually.

10 Circulate to monitor, prompt and help. Encourage individual pupils to say the words aloud as they work.

11 Correct the exercise collectively.

Key
1 'o' for bottle: John, log, on, frog
2 'ou' for trousers: round, sound, cow, how
3 'oo' for goose: juice, two, shoe, zoo

Extension
Ask pupils to identify the pairs of rhyming words from each section and to make a list of them.

Diddle diddle dumpling flashcard

1 **Colour the bottle orange.**
Write the letter.

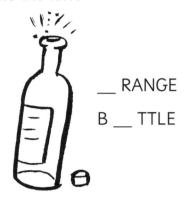

__ RANGE

B __ TTLE

If the word has 'o' for 'bottle',
colour the circle orange.

John	moon	book	log
 spoon	on	 frog	 look

2 **Colour the trousers brown.**
Write the letters.

BR __ __ N
TR __ __ SERS

If the word has 'ou' for 'trousers',
colour the circle brown.

door	round	four	toe
 sound	 cow	 no	how

3 **Colour the goose blue.**
Write the letters.

BL __ E
G __ __ SE

If the word has 'oo' for 'goose',
colour the circle blue.

plum	juice	drum	one
 two	shoe	sun	 zoo

PRIMARY ACTIVITY BOX

8.1

Farmyard fun

ACTIVITY TYPE
song, whole class dictation, pairwork activity

LANGUAGE FOCUS
farm animals
there is …/there are …
has got

LEVEL
1

AGE RANGE
5–8

SKILLS
listening, speaking, writing (optional)

TIME
60 minutes

MATERIALS
one (enlarged) copy of the *Farmyard fun* flashcard, a copy of the *Farmyard fun* worksheet per pupil, a sheet of blank paper per pupil, crayons, scissors, glue, cassette (optional)

Before class

Make a copy of the *Farmyard fun* worksheet for each pupil. Make an enlarged copy of the flashcard and colour it attractively. If you have a large class, you might also want to make a copy of the flashcard for each pupil so that everyone will be able to see it clearly.

In class

1 Show the class the flashcard and say, *Look, he's Old MacDonald.* Talk about the picture, practising key vocabulary: *farm, farm animals,* etc. Ask questions about the picture, e.g. *What's his name? Where is he? What is this animal? What's this? Where's the fox?* Revise or pre-teach *duck, cow, sheep, horse* and *pig.*

2 Play the cassette or sing from the tapescript.

Tapescript

Old MacDonald had a farm, A-E-I-O-U
And on that farm he had a cow, A-E-I-O-U
With a moo-moo here, and a moo-moo there,
Here a moo, there a moo, everywhere a moo-moo.
Old MacDonald had a farm, A-E-I-O-U.

Horse: *neigh-neigh*
Duck: *quack-quack*
Sheep: *baa-baa*
Pig: *oink-oink*

3 Pupils repeat the first verse line by line and then stand up and sing the whole song.

4 Give pupils a copy of *Farmyard fun* and ask them to colour the animals according to your instructions, e.g. *Colour the pigs pink. Colour the cows black and white.*

5 Pupils cut out their animals. Young children need only cut roughly around the shapes.

6 Give pupils a blank piece of paper and tell them this is their farmyard. Ask them to draw a farmhouse in one corner of the sheet using simple instructions, e.g.
Draw a square. This is your house. In the house draw a door and four windows …
Do not ask them to colour the farmyard yet, as this stops the glue sticking later.

7 Dictate which animals are in their farmyard, allowing pupils time to place each animal on their sheet. Use the structure most suitable for your group, i.e.
On your farm you have got a dog and two hens OR
On your farm there are two cats, there's one horse, etc.

8 Arrange pupils into pairs. Demonstrate the activity by example. One pupil selects animals for his farm in secret and then dictates to the other pupil using the same structure as the teacher in step 7. The second pupil places the animals onto the sheet. When they have finished they compare their farms and then change roles.

9 Pupils stick a selection of animals onto their sheet and then colour the background. These farmyard pictures can then be displayed.

Extension

For more advanced pupils, in step 6 you could ask them also to draw a field next to the house and a pond in the bottom corner, so that in step 7 you could dictate, for example, *There are three ducks on the pond. There are two cows in the field.*

Optional written work

Pupils can write a description of their own farmyard using the structures they have practised.

PHOTOCOPIABLE From *Primary Activity Box* by C. Nixon and M. Tomlinson © Cambridge University Press 2001

Two little dicky birds

ACTIVITY TYPE
rhyme with puppets: whole class and pairwork

LANGUAGE FOCUS
classroom instructions

LEVEL
1

AGE RANGE
6–9

SKILLS
listening, speaking

TIME
50 minutes

MATERIALS
a copy of the *Two little dicky birds* worksheet per pupil, crayons, string, scissors, glue, cassette (optional)

Before class
Prepare two flapping birds to show the class before starting the task. Make a copy of the *Two little dicky birds* worksheet for each pupil.

In class
1 Hold up the two birds you have made to show the class. Say *This is Peter. This is Paul. They are birds. Look and listen.* Play the cassette or read the tapescript, doing the actions with the birds.

Tapescript	*Actions*
Two little dicky birds Sitting on a wall,	Sit the two birds in front of you on a table.
One called Peter,	Hold up one bird.
One called Paul.	Hold up the other bird.
Fly away, Peter.	Make 'Peter' fly away behind your back.
Fly away, Paul.	Make 'Paul' fly away behind your back.
Come back, Peter.	Make 'Peter' come back.
Come back, Paul.	Make 'Paul' come back.

2 Say *Listen and repeat.* Play the cassette or read the tapescript and pupils repeat the rhyme line by line. Check for pronunciation difficulties and correct if necessary.

3 Before the class repeat the rhyme again, give them each a copy of the worksheet and ask them to make their birds. Demonstrate each step for pupils to follow. Try to use English as much as possible when you give the instructions.
   a Fold the photocopy along the folding line (the base of the bird).
   b Colour the bird.
   c Cut out the bird. It is important *not* to cut along the folding line so that the two sides of the bird are still joined.
   d Stick the head and body together, taking care not to stick the wings.
   e Colour the inside of the wings and open them out so they flap.
   f Thread string through the tips of the wings to make a bird mobile.

4 Organise pupils into pairs, and tell one pupil to be Peter and the other to be Paul. They can write the name on their bird if they like. Repeat the rhyme again, this time with pupils doing the actions with the birds they have just made. One pupil does the actions for Peter, the other for Paul.

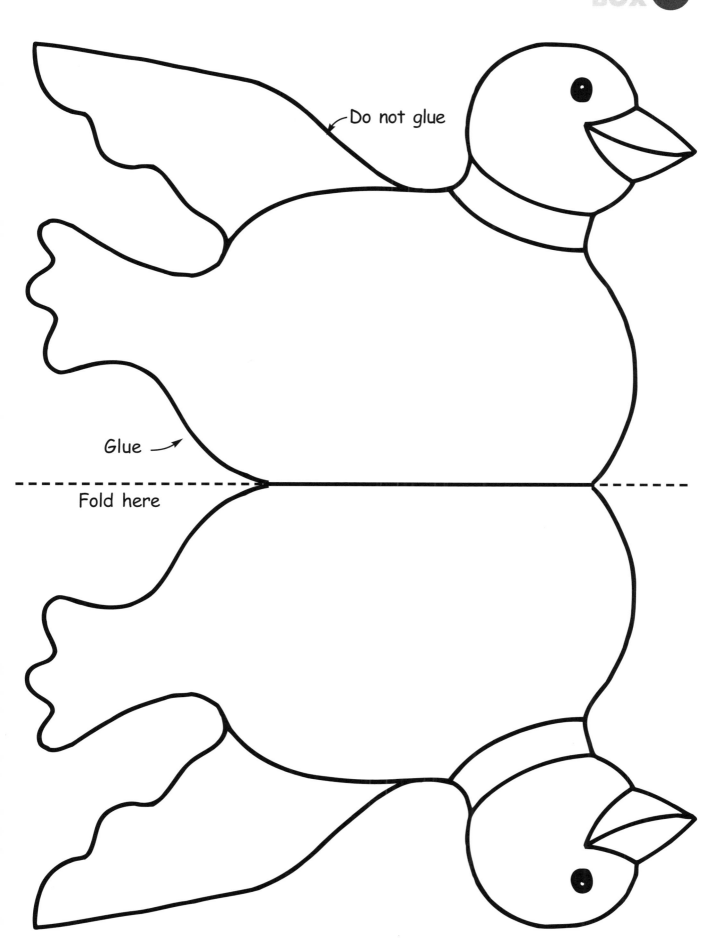

Do not glue

Glue

Fold here

8.3 PRIMARY ACTIVITY BOX

Chatterboxes

ACTIVITY TYPE
individual 'make and do' activity, pairwork

LANGUAGE FOCUS
numbers 1–10
colours
basic adjectives and nouns
as for comparisons

LEVEL
3

AGE RANGE
8–11

SKILLS
writing, listening, speaking

TIME
45 minutes

MATERIALS
a copy of the *Chatterboxes* worksheet per pupil, scissors, crayons

Before class

Make a copy of the *Chatterboxes* worksheet for each pupil. Prepare a *Chatterbox* (see worksheet and step 6 below) and choose an object that will illustrate a particular adjective, e.g. a flower (as beautiful as a flower).

In class

1 Hold the flower up and say *For me a flower is beautiful*. Write **as** beautiful **as** *a flower* on the blackboard, highlighting *as* and *as* to draw pupils' attention to the structure to be practised.

2 Write *as big as …* on the board to elicit different suggestions, e.g. *an elephant, a house, a whale*, etc. Do the same with some more adjectives, e.g. *tall, small, heavy,* to 'warm up' your pupils and establish a creative flow. Do not censor your pupils' ideas unless they make an unfavourable comparison with another pupil. In this case make it very clear that this sort of comparison is not allowed and ask the offender to say 'sorry'.

3 Ask your pupils to write eight similar phrases in their notebooks, using a different adjective each time. If necessary, you could give them a list such as: *tall, short, fat, thin, clever, stupid, ugly, beautiful*. Tell them to keep their work secret. Set a time limit. Circulate to monitor and correct.

4 Demonstrate how the *Chatterbox* works. Ask a pupil to come to the front, hold out your *Chatterbox* and say *Choose a number*. When the pupil selects the number, count while opening and closing the 'mouth' by stretching your thumbs and index fingers alternately outwards horizontally and vertically in the shape of a cross. Stop at the selected number and say *What's your favourite colour?* Repeat the process while spelling out the colour. When you finish spelling, say *Choose a colour*. Open the flap of that colour to reveal the 'secret message' and read it aloud. Thank your pupil and ask him or her to sit down.

5 Give out the worksheets and ask pupils to follow the instructions to make the *Chatterbox*.

6 Then ask them to do the following, demonstrating as you go along:
   a In words, write a number between one and ten on each square flap.
   b Open out the *Chatterbox* into a square again and colour each of the eight triangles inside a different colour.
   c Write their eight sentences under the eight coloured triangles, starting the sentence with *You're …*. Tell them that these are 'secret messages' and not to let their neighbours see them. Set a time limit.

7 Pupils move around the classroom with their finished *Chatterboxes* and carry out the activity with as many different partners as time allows. Circulate to monitor and correct. Pay special attention to the instruction *Choose* and the correct spelling of the colours. Some of the comparative sentences may be mildly offensive, but it is precisely this element, the chance of 'innocently' being rude to each other, that most children enjoy enormously.

Options

This activity can also be used to practise giving and receiving personal information, e.g. *How old are you? What's your name? Where are you from?* etc., asking simple questions, e.g. *What colour's an elephant? Where's your book? How much is 5 and 4?* etc., or simple sentence formation with adjectives, e.g. *You're beautiful. You're clever. You're tall*, etc. For more proficient learners the *Chatterboxes* can be used for fortune telling and predicting using future tenses, e.g. *You're going to be rich*, etc.

1 Cut out the square.

2 Fold the corners into the centre along the dotted lines. (a)

3 Turn the paper over (folded side down) and fold the corners into the centre. (b and c)

4 Fold in half to form a rectangle with two squares on the outside. Then open it up and fold it again the other way. (d)

5 Put your thumbs and forefingers under the square flaps (e) and join them in the middle (f).

a 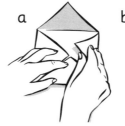 b   c

d   e   f

PRIMARY ACTIVITY BOX

8.4 Days and dates

ACTIVITY TYPE
rhyme, individual 'make and do' activity

LANGUAGE FOCUS
days and months
numbers

LEVEL
2

AGE RANGE
8–11

SKILLS
listening, writing

TIME
50 minutes

MATERIALS
one piece of coloured A4 card per pupil, scissors, glue, spare pictures or postcards, crayons, hole punch, two copies of the *Days and dates* worksheet per pupil, coloured wool or thread, a calendar of the next year for reference, cassette (optional)

Before class

Prepare a *Days and dates* calendar to show the class before starting the task.

Make two copies of the *Days and dates* worksheet for each pupil. They can be enlarged copies if you wish.

Before the class ask your pupils to bring a nice picture (no bigger than half A4) from a magazine or a postcard that they would like to use to decorate their calendar.

In class

1 Pre-teach or revise the months.

2 Play the cassette or read the tapescript.

> *Tapescript*
>
> 30 days have September,
> April, June and November.
> All the rest have 31
> Excepting February alone,
> And that has 28 days clear,
> And 29 in each leap year.

3 Pupils repeat the rhyme line by line. Check for pronunciation difficulties and correct if necessary.

4 Ask pupils *How many days are there in each month?* (Tell them how many days February has for the next year.)

5 Give out the photocopies and coloured card and tell pupils to write the names of the months in pencil on the second line of the calendar. The month of January must be written in the box without the instructions 'Stick here'. Demonstrate by example if necessary – the J is given in the correct place for *January* and *July*.

6 They then write the numbers 1–30 or 1–31, depending on the month, in vertical columns, starting on the first square in each calendar month. When they have done this, check collectively that they have got the right number of days for each month and that they have written them in the right squares.

7 Tell them which day of the week falls on 1st January (not necessarily a Monday) and ask them to write that day on the first left-hand line next to 1, 8, 15, 22, 29.

8 Pupils write the rest of the days of the week for the rest of the year and cut out the months. (Be careful – not all the months will start on a Monday.)

9 Pupils stick their pictures on the top half of the card and the month of December immediately below it.

10 They then put glue along the *Stick here* line and stick the month of *November* over the top. Repeat the process with the other calendar months *October, September,* etc. until finally *January* is on the top. Demonstrate by example to ensure that pupils stick only on the *Stick here* line.

11 Pupils punch two holes at the top of each calendar and thread it with a piece of wool so that it can be hung up.

12 If there is time pupils can decorate the months by colouring special days or dates, (family birthdays, national or local public holidays, etc.). They can also write over the month and day names in crayons or felt-tip pens.

For more practice on days and dates see **9.4 Broken words**

Days and dates

	Stick here					
J						
	1					
	2					

Stick here				Stick here			

Stick here				Stick here			

MAKE AND DO

8.5 PRIMARY ACTIVITY BOX

Dress me up

ACTIVITY TYPE
whole class dictation
pairwork information gap

LANGUAGE FOCUS
clothes
colours
possessive 's
is wearing/has got
his, her

LEVEL
1

AGE RANGE
5–9

SKILLS
listening, speaking, writing
(optional)

TIME
60 minutes

MATERIALS
a copy of the *Dress me up*
worksheet and a sheet of
blank paper per pupil,
crayons, scissors, glue

Before class
Make a copy of the *Dress me up* worksheet for each pupil.

In class
1 Give pupils a copy of the *Dress me up* worksheet. Check that they know the names of all the clothes.

2 Ask pupils to colour the clothes according to your instructions, e.g.
Colour one T-shirt blue and one T-shirt yellow, etc.
Note: this allows you to decide upon the vocabulary names you want to choose (e.g. *jumper, sweater, pullover, jersey*).

3 Pupils cut out the boy and girl and the articles of clothing.

4 Now tell the class what the boy and girl are wearing. The idea is for pupils to place clothes as you dictate. You can decide which structure is most suitable for your class:
Lilian's got (pink) shorts.
Lilian's wearing (pink) shorts.
Lilian's shorts are (pink).

5 Arrange pupils into pairs. Demonstrate the activity by example. One pupil dresses the models in secret and then dictates to the other pupil using the same structure as the teacher in step 4. The second pupil places the clothes onto the model. When they have finished they compare their outfits. They then change roles.

Option
For younger pupils, instead of dividing the class into pairs, one pupil can dictate the clothes to the rest of the class for them to dress their models.

Optional written work
Pupils stick their models into their notebooks, or onto a piece of paper. They then stick the clothes on and write a description of the boy and girl and the clothes they are wearing, using the structures they have practised.

For more practice on possessives and clothes see **5.6 Colour co-ordinates 6.5 Cowboy dot-to-dot 7.1 Jack and Jill**

Dress me up

9.1

PRIMARY ACTIVITY BOX

DIY wordsearch

ACTIVITY TYPE
individual or group
wordsearch activity

LANGUAGE FOCUS
any lexical groups

LEVEL
1–3

AGE RANGE
8–11

SKILLS
reading, writing

TIME
30–40 minutes depending on
the target number of words

MATERIALS
a copy of the *DIY wordsearch*
worksheet per pupil or per
group of two to four pupils,
an enlarged completed
wordsearch or OHT

Before class
Make a copy of the *DIY wordsearch* worksheet for each pupil or for each group of two to four pupils. Prepare an enlarged and completed wordsearch to show to your class before doing the task.

In class
1 Explain that pupils are going to create a wordsearch. Show them an example by drawing a reduced grid on the board and writing three words, one letter per square, in different directions: horizontally, vertically and diagonally. Now fill in the remaining squares with random letters so that the original three words are hidden. Explain that all the letters must look the same (all either capitals or lower case) so that the hidden words don't look different.

2 Divide pupils into small groups. Give each group a photocopy and ask them to write their names at the top.

3 Tell them they must choose one or more lexical group. You can give them options to choose from: parts of the body, animals, hobbies, clothes, etc., depending on their level and what you have covered in class. Groups should choose different areas. They write this area at the top of their sheet in the space provided and can do a small picture to illustrate it if they wish.

4 Pupils write their words in the chart. They try to write as many as possible in a limited time period, fifteen minutes for example. Pupils count the number of words they have and write this information in the space provided. Alternatively you can give them a target number of words, twenty for example.

5 Give them five more minutes to fill in the remaining spaces using any random letters of the alphabet.

6 Draw their attention to your enlarged wordsearch and circle three of the hidden words.

7 Pupils exchange sheets and find and circle the words which the other groups have written.

Optional written work
Pupils write the words below the chart and use these words to make sentences according to their knowledge and ability. For example:

hat: *It's a green hat.*
They've got green hats.
He's wearing a green hat.
She wore a green hat yesterday.

For more practice on word formation see **3.7 Word scramble**

DIY wordsearch

Theme(s): _____

Number of words: _____

Names: _____

_____

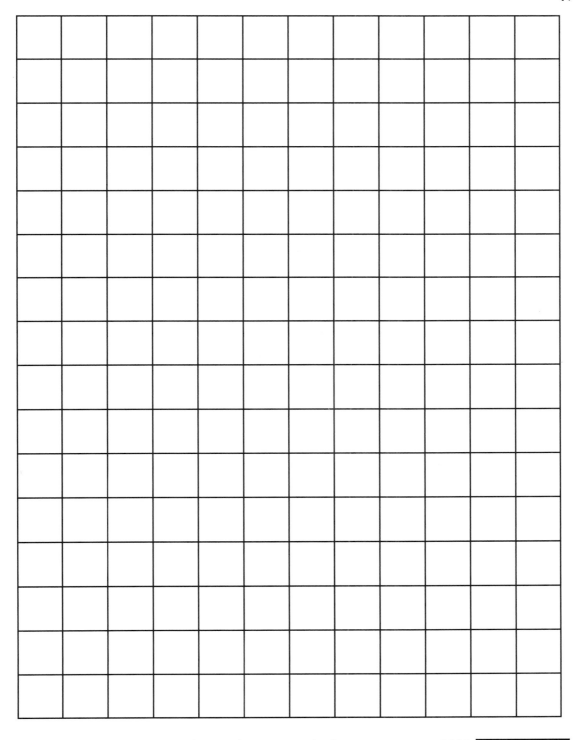

PRIMARY ACTIVITY BOX

Where are they sitting?

ACTIVITY TYPE
individual cognitive puzzle, information transfer

LANGUAGE FOCUS
can
prepositions *next to, between on someone's left/right*

LEVEL
2

AGE RANGE
9–11

SKILLS
reading for information, writing, listening (optional)

TIME
30 minutes

MATERIALS
a copy of the *Where are they sitting?* worksheet per pupil

Before class
Make a copy of the *Where are they sitting?* worksheet for each pupil.

In class
1 Pre-teach or revise the verbs and the prepositions on the worksheet.

2 Explain what the diagram represents. Draw a circle on the board and say *This is a table.* Divide this circle into five segments and say *There are five people around the table.* Choose five pupils' names from the class and write them in the sections.

3 Draw another circle around this and write *can* in it, and then an outer circle and write *can't* in it. Ask the five pupils whose names you have chosen some 'can' questions, e.g.
Can you play the violin?
Can you ride a horse?
Can you run?
According to whether they answer *Yes* or *No*, write the appropriate verb in the *can* or *can't* circle in the section of the diagram with the pupil's name. Only write the corresponding verb in each space; the complete sentence should not be written. You should now have a completed diagram similar to the one on p. 127.

4 Give pupils the worksheet. They complete the spaces by reading the information below. Be prepared to allow them sufficient time without interfering if possible. Circulate to help and monitor.

Key
The answer key is given on p. 127.

Option
Instead of giving pupils the diagram with the written text, give them a worksheet with just the diagram and dictate the six numbered sentences. Pupils check between themselves, then dictate the sentences back to you. Write the sentences on the board to ensure that all the pupils have a correct copy to work from. They then proceed as above.

Optional written work
1 Once pupils have completed the information, they write a sentence for each person. This can also serve as a good opportunity to practise the use of *but*, e.g.
David can ride a bike, but he can't swim.

2 Some pupils can write their sentences on the board. Correct this collectively and give pupils time to correct their own sentences.

For more practice on *can* see **5.3 They can do it**

Where are they sitting?

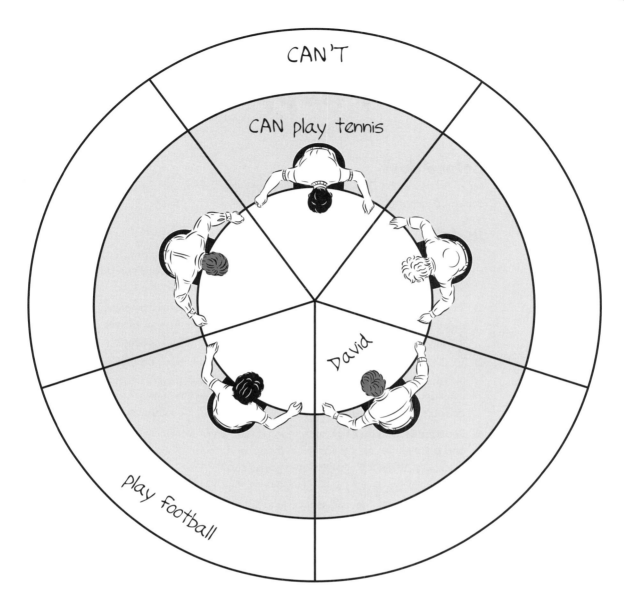

1 Sarah is on David's left, and Mary is on David's right.

2 One boy can play tennis, but he can't play the piano.
   The girl next to him can draw, but can't dance.

3 John is sitting next to Mary.

4 Jim is next to Sarah.

5 The person between Mary and Sarah can ride a bike, but he can't swim.

6 The man next to John can drive a car, but he can't sing.

7 The girl next to Jim can do maths, but she can't play football.

9.3

Dotty's puppies

ACTIVITY TYPE
individual cognitive puzzle, information transfer

LANGUAGE FOCUS
have got
parts of the body
adjectives *long, short, fat, thin, big, small*

LEVEL
3

AGE RANGE
9–11

SKILLS
reading, writing, listening, speaking (optional)

TIME
45 minutes

MATERIALS
a copy of the *Dotty's puppies* worksheet per pupil

Before class
Make a copy of the *Dotty's puppies* worksheet for each pupil. If you are able, make an OHT copy of the chart.

In class
1 Write *Dotty is a Dalmatian dog* on the board, say *She's got five puppies.* Explain that puppies are baby dogs. Give out the photocopies. Ask pupils to read the information in silence while you copy the chart onto the board or project the OHT.

2 When they have finished reading, draw pupils' attention to the chart and read the first piece of information on the worksheet aloud. Point to the row **name** and show them that the information about each puppy is organised in vertical columns.

3 To illustrate that the information is not in progressive order, point to the word **Lucky** and move your finger along the top row with a questioning expression, shrugging your shoulders, or write question marks in the spaces for the names if you prefer. Say *It's not possible* and encourage pupils to continue reading the information.

4 Read the second piece of information aloud. Say *Aha! Basket number one.* Look excited and point to the second column in the second row as though you have made a great discovery. Write the information onto the chart.

5 Continue to explain by example and when you feel that pupils have got a clear idea of what they have to do and seem confident, ask them to complete the puzzle individually.

6 While the class are doing the puzzle, circulate to help and correct. Try not to give them too much help, only prompting and suggesting.

7 Correct the activity collectively. Ask pupils to read the information back to you, point by point, while you write it on the blackboard. Encourage them to justify their answers.

Key

Name	Lucky	Bright	Shiny	Little	Twinkle
basket number	2	1	4	5	3
long or short legs?	long	short	long	short	short
fat or thin body?	fat	thin	fat	thin	fat
big or small ears?	big	small	small	small	big
boy or girl?	girl	boy	girl	boy	girl

Extension – Quiz
Give two points for a correct answer, one for an answer that contains the correct answer but is grammatically incorrect, and if this is the case, a bonus point to the pupil who can give the grammatically correct answer. Keep a running total on the board, and deduct points for shouting out the answer or rowdiness. You can also do the quiz in teams or pairs.

Questions
1 How many puppies has Dotty got?
2 Where's Shiny?
3 Has Bright got a black mark on his head?
4 How many puppies are boys?
5 Is Twinkle in basket number three?

6 Has Little got big or small ears?
7 How many puppies have got fat bodies?
8 Where's Lucky?
9 Are Twinkle's eyes closed?
10 Which basket is Little in?

For more practice on *have got* + physical description see **5.2 Identikit**

Dotty's puppies

Read the sentences and fill in the chart.

1 Dotty's got five puppies. Two are boys and three are girls. Their names are Twinkle, Little, Lucky, Shiny and Bright.

2 The puppy in basket number one has got short legs and small ears.

3 Two puppies have got thin bodies. They're in baskets one and five.

4 Lucky's got long legs and big ears.

5 Three puppies have got short legs.

6 Bright's got short legs and small ears. He isn't in basket number five.

7 Only two puppies have got big ears and they've got fat bodies too.

8 Little's got short legs and small ears, but he isn't in basket number one.

9 The puppy with short legs and big ears isn't in basket number two. Her name's Twinkle.

10 The puppy in basket number four has got long legs and a fat body. Her name isn't Lucky.

name	Lucky				
basket number		1			
long or short legs?			long		
fat or thin body?				thin	
big or small ears?					big
boy or girl?	girl				

Write the puppies' names on the baskets.

Broken words

ACTIVITY TYPE
individual vocabulary
matching activity

LANGUAGE FOCUS
vocabulary: months, days,
seasons

LEVEL
2

AGE RANGE
8–11

SKILLS
reading, writing

TIME
40 minutes

MATERIALS
a copy of the *Broken words*
worksheet per pupil

Before class
Make a copy of the *Broken Words* worksheet for each pupil.

In class

1 Revise or pre-teach the necessary vocabulary (see Key below for the list of words). This can be done using time prepositions or ordinal numbers e.g.
Which month is after February? What day of the week is before Wednesday?
Which is the third month?

2 Give each pupil a copy of the *Broken words* worksheet.

3 Explain the task by example on the board:
Write *Mon* _____

_____

on the board, and a number of word endings (*ne, vember, sday, day, tumn, th, key*) each inside a box similar to those on the worksheet.

4 Ask pupils to connect the beginning with the ending. You can suggest possible alternatives for them to say *Yes* or *No*, e.g.
Is it Monvember? Is it Monsday? Is it Monday?
When they get the correct answer write the complete word on the line next to *Mon* (Monday) and cross out 'day'. It is important for pupils to understand that the first part of the word is only a prompt and that they must write the complete word on the line.

5 Explain that there are two lines because there are two different words which start with Mon. Continue with the procedure as above until pupils get the second answer (Monkey).

6 Circulate to monitor, but try to encourage pupil autonomy; do not tell them answers but rather prompt and suggest.

7 When pupils have completed the task, ask them to correct it first by comparing their sheets in small groups, and if necessary as a class–teacher dictation on the board.

Key

1 Monday, Monkey	10 Thursday, Thanks
2 May, March	11 Friday, Friend
3 Autumn, August	12 Saturday, Sandwich
4 October, Octopus	13 Sunday, Sunny
5 November, Nothing	14 Tuesday, Train
6 June, Jump	15 April, Apple
7 September, Seven	16 January, Jam
8 December, Dentist	17 February, Feet
9 Wednesday, Weather	

Note

There is a *Broken words* template on p. 125 so that you can repeat this activity to practise different lexical areas.

For more practice on days and months see **8.4 Days and dates**

Broken words

Find the words, days, months and seasons.

Example:

Ju   July
          Jug

1 Mon _____

2 Ma _____

3 Au _____

4 Octo _____

5 No _____

6 Ju _____

7 Se _____

8 De _____

9 We _____

10 Th _____

11 Fr _____

12 Sa _____

13 Sun _____

14 T _____

15 Ap _____

16 Ja _____

17 Fe _____

thing   ptember

ather   g ✔   gust

ndwich

ber   cember

day   turday   ntist

y   ven   day

iday   rch

tumn

bruary

ne   pus

ursday

mp

vember

iend

ly ✔   ny

rain

ril   uesday

ple   m   nuary   et

key   anks   dnesday

9.5

PRIMARY ACTIVITY BOX

Shaping up

ACTIVITY TYPE
individual information transfer activity

LANGUAGE FOCUS
comparatives and superlatives
shapes
colours
in, inside, this, the other

LEVEL
3

AGE RANGE
9–11

SKILLS
reading or listening, writing (optional)

TIME
30 minutes

MATERIALS
a copy of the *Shaping up* worksheet with or without the written text (see options) per pupil, crayons, cassette (optional)

Before class

Make a copy of the *Shaping up* worksheet for each pupil.

In class

1 Revise or pre-teach the necessary vocabulary and grammar.

Reading option

1 Give each pupil a copy of *Shaping up* with the written text. Ask them to read the text and colour the diagram.

2 Circulate to monitor, but try to encourage pupil autonomy; do not tell them answers but rather prompt and suggest.

Listening option

1 Give each pupil a copy of *Shaping up* without the written text.

2 Play the cassette or read the tapescript, pausing after each sentence to allow pupils time to colour the diagram.

Tapescript

There are three stars. The biggest one is yellow, and the smallest one is blue. The star in a triangle is red. This triangle is green. The smallest triangle is red, but the triangle inside the circle is orange.

There are two rectangles. The brown one is longer than the grey one. The biggest circle is pink, and the smallest circle is black. The other circle is yellow.

There are two squares. One is white, and the other is purple. The purple square is smaller than the white one.

3 When pupils have completed the task, ask them to correct it by comparing their sheets in small groups.

Optional written work

1 Ask pupils to draw a set number of shapes (ten for example) of different sizes on a sheet of paper.

2 Ask them to write instructions to colour the shapes underneath their diagram.

3 It is a good idea to collect these sheets for correction before using them with other pupils in another lesson.

For more practice on prepositions see **5.4 Room for improvement 3.4 Colourful cans**

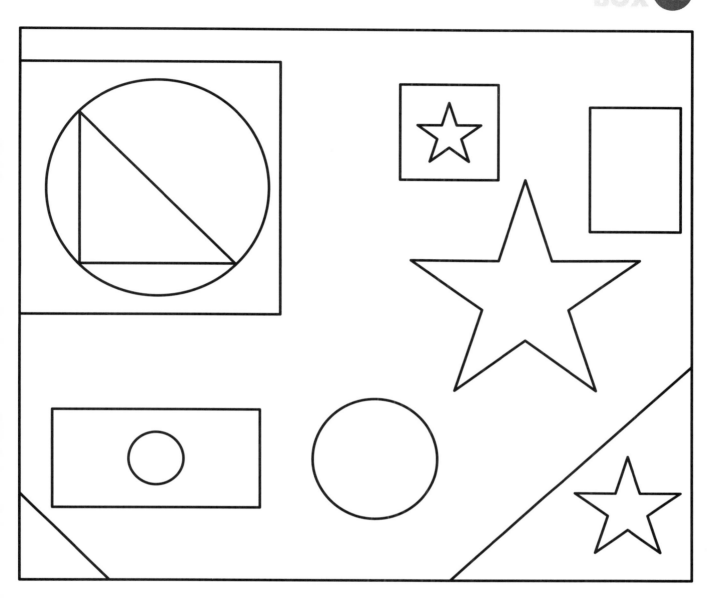

Read the text and colour the shapes.

There are three stars. The biggest one is yellow, and the smallest one is blue. The star in a triangle is red. This triangle is green. The smallest triangle is red, but the triangle inside the circle is orange.

There are two rectangles. The brown one is longer than the grey one. The biggest circle is pink, and the smallest circle is black. The other circle is yellow.

There are two squares. One is white, and the other is purple. The purple square is smaller than the white one.

PRIMARY ACTIVITY BOX

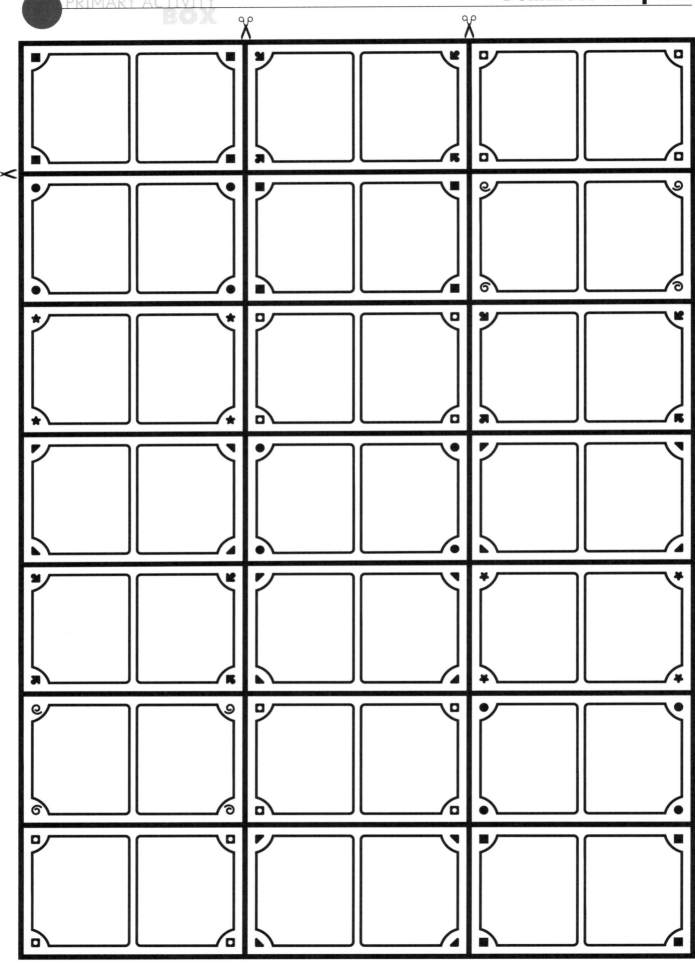

 From *Primary Activity Box* by C. Nixon and M. Tomlinson © Cambridge University Press 2001

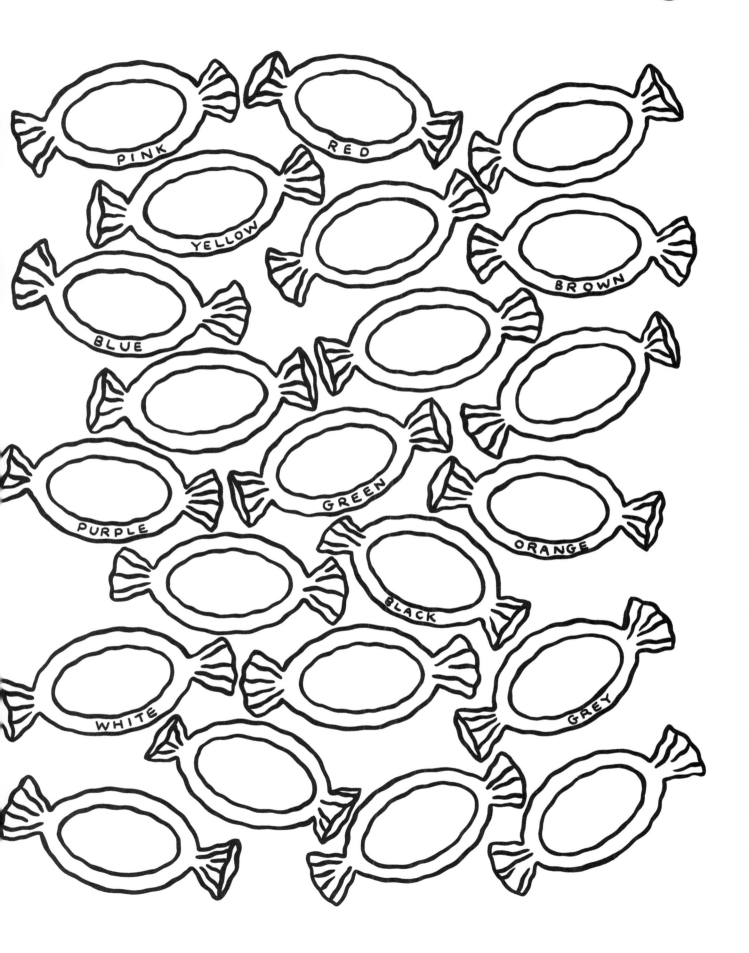

PRIMARY ACTIVITY BOX

TEACHER'S BASEBOARD

Broken words template

Example:

1
2
3
4
5
6
7
8
9
10
11
12
13
14
15
16
17

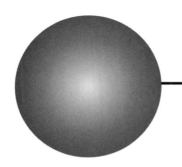

Key

2.5 ABC crossword

4.3 Fabulous phonicolours

mouth	brown	head	red	down	brown
queen	green	go	yellow	close	yellow
fish	pink	stop	orange	desk	red
toe	yellow	skirt	purple	man	black
egg	red	eight	grey	time	white
word	purple	big	pink	knee	green
see	green	bike	white	clock	orange
two	blue	cat	black	ten	red
apple	black	coat	yellow	six	pink
moon	blue	zoo	blue	hand	black
play	grey	dress	red	nine	white
eye	white	cake	grey	girl	purple
hop	orange	house	brown	room	blue
nose	yellow	shirt	purple	me	green

Key

7.3 Lucy Locket

lock	door	turn	key
body	morning	purple	queen
bottle	four	dirty	we
stop	horse	bird	cheese
box	sport	shirt	jeans
clock	daughter	thirty	eat
hot	north	circle	teeth
fox	water	her	clean
sock	short	Thursday	three

9.2 Where are they sitting?

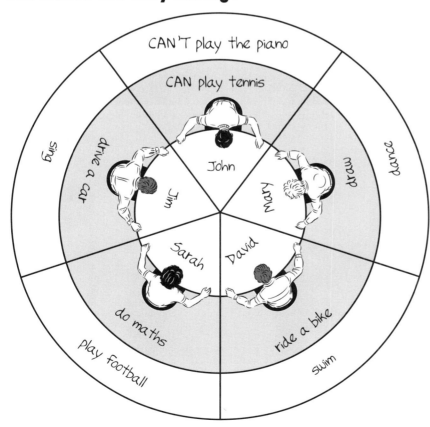

From *Primary Activity Box* by C. Nixon and M. Tomlinson © Cambridge University Press 2001 **PHOTOCOPIABLE** **127**

Actions for Incy Wincy Spider song

a

Incy Wincy Spider climbed up the spout.

b
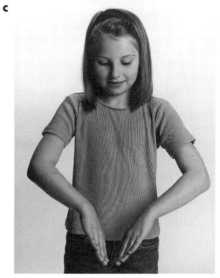
Down came the rain ...

c
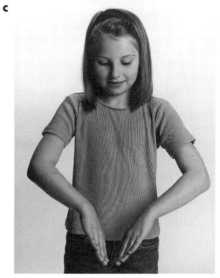
... and washed poor Incy out.

d

Out came the sunshine ...

e

... and dried up all the rain.

f
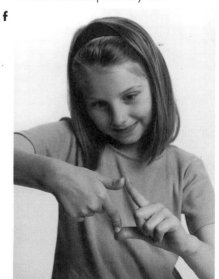
So Incy Wincy Spider climbed up the spout again.

Actions for Lucy Locket rhyme

a

b

c